21ˢᵗ Century Writing

An accelerated program to help students develop their writing skills

Written by Paul Fleisher, Donna Fout and Mary Ann Ready

Illustrated by Alex Glikin

Teaching & Learning Company

1204 Buchanan St., P.O. Box 10
Carthage, IL 62321-0010

This book belongs to

____

Acknowledgements

Over the years, many educators have shared their good ideas—and the good ideas they'd borrowed from others—with us. We would like to express our thanks to all our colleagues who, directly or indirectly, helped us generate ideas from which the activities in *21st Century Writing* grew. We owe a great debt of gratitude to them, and to the spirit of sharing and cooperation that characterizes our profession.

Thanks to Anna Lou Aaroe, Debra Fleisher, John Hunter, Gregg Neylan and Susan Stebbins for contributing ideas that have been included in this book. We would also like to thank Dr. Deborah Jewell-Sherman, superintendent of Richmond Public Schools; Dr. Margaret Jones, former principal of Binford Middle School; Catherine Rosenbaum, Reading and Language Arts Specialist, Virginia Department of Education; and Rodney Fout, Coordinator of Programs for the Gifted, Richmond Public Schools for supporting this project from its inception.

Cover design by Jennifer Morgan

Table of Contents

Dear Teacher or Parent,

Writing skills are more important than ever. Most of the information flashing around our planet at the speed of light still originates as written words. New technologies have created a world in which more printed material is being published than ever before. People still want to express themselves through essays, stories, poems and plays. And no matter what career we choose, virtually all of us must communicate and record our efforts in writing—even if our words are stored and transmitted electronically. Clearly, 21st century students still need to become competent writers.

Writing is a craft. Using the raw materials of our language—words, sentence structure and logic—writers work to form well-designed, aesthetically pleasing compositions. And, like any craft, the quality of a person's work improves with practice. The only way to improve one's writing skills is to write. The activities in *21st Century Writing* are intended to help students develop their craftsmanship and their sense that writing can be a satisfying means of self-expression.

Although the activities in *21st Century Writing* are presented in a series of separate chapters, we don't expect teachers to proceed directly through the curriculum in the order of presentation. Use the activities in the order that best meets the needs of your students.

Sincerely,

Paul Fleisher, Donna Fout and Mary Ann Ready

1. Revising and rewriting is an essential part of the writing process.

No written product is finished after only one draft. The only way to create a polished piece of writing is to revise and rewrite. Make revision and rewriting a regular part of your instructional process. Remind students that revising is much more than simply checking for spelling and grammatical errors, or just rewriting the same words in their best handwriting.

Revising can be overwhelming to students, especially if they are given the task of rewriting without sufficient guidance. To make matters worse, they have to do it after they think they've already "finished" writing. But as students confer with peers and teachers about their work, they will begin to see areas where a reader may have understood something completely different from what was intended. Students will soon discover the value of revising as their writing becomes clearer and they are more able to express their ideas precisely. As a result, they'll begin to produce more satisfactory, and more satisfying products.

Teach the acronym CARES (Change, Add, Rearrange, Eliminate and Standardize) to give students a simple structure to organize their revisions. *21st Century Writing* includes a number of exercises intended to give students practice using this structure. Of course, the ultimate goal is to extend those methods to their own original writings.

You are your students' most important editor. If your students know you believe writing is important, they will adopt a similar attitude. Don't hesitate to suggest ways for students to correct or improve their work. After all, you are the most experienced writer in the classroom. Remember, professional editors take similar steps with the work of experienced professional writers.

By serving as editors, teachers show respect for students' work. We also model the behaviors and attitudes we want students to develop as they revise their own work independently. Editing also helps students produce polished work, which generates pride and satisfaction.

If students write and receive little feedback, they begin to lose interest in making their work better. Teachers cannot always work one-on-one with students during the writing process, so don't be afraid to write comments, questions and compliments on drafts. Even a note saying, "Talk to me about this paragraph," lets students know you have read their work carefully and that you care enough to help them produce polished work.

Make sure students know that in many cases, your editing suggestions are recommendations only. Except for instances of standardizing spelling, grammar, punctuation and sentence structure, students should feel that it's okay to write their own way if they don't prefer the teacher's suggestions. We want them to express their own ideas in their own voices.

Editing one's own work is quite difficult. Since a writer already knows what he or she intended to say, finding even the simplest typographical errors while rereading can be a challenge. That's why editing assistance from peers is so important.

Many of the activities in this book are designed to be taught using a "writers' workshop" approach. After students have written a draft, they should exchange their work with a partner or small group of classmates and get feedback. They then use that feedback to revise and create an improved draft or final product. Make sure students team with a variety of different partners. Otherwise they'll get the same kind of feedback over and over again.

Occasionally allow students to present an unedited draft by reading it aloud to a group. The writer will catch and correct many errors as he or she reads it. Allow time for comment and discussion of each piece after it is read. It is important to create an atmosphere in which students feel safe to share their writing. Remember, each piece of writing is an extension of the writer, and it takes courage to share. Be sure to let students know that you appreciate their willingness to open themselves to comment.

Students will need guidance in giving good feedback. Here are some pointers to share with the class:

—As editor, tell the writer about both things he or she did well, and things that need improvement.

—Look beyond spelling, grammar and punctuation. There are more important ways to improve almost every piece of writing (such as composition and style).

—As much as possible, use "I statements" in your feedback. For example, instead of "This doesn't make any sense," you might say, "I don't understand what you're trying to explain here," or "I'm having trouble understanding this sentence."

—The most useful feedback is specific. For example, "This sentence sounds funny," is not as helpful as, "This sentence has a plural subject and a singular verb."

Of course, peer editing doesn't take the place of teacher editing conferences. If teachers are to convince students that editing is essential, we must be a significant part of the process. Once the class is working on an assignment, it's a good idea to move from student to student, reading their work and discussing their ideas.

By holding editing conferences with students, you let them know your expectations. Students will learn by your example. When a teacher gives clear, straightforward, specific feedback, students will follow that model. They will learn to provide useful feedback to their classmates, and develop the ability to analyze and critique their own work as well. With practice, the editing process will become more familiar and less threatening.

Early in the year, give students copies of "Writers' Workshop: Tips for Helping One Another Become Better Writers" (in Chapter 1: Revising and Rewriting). Review the workshop process with them, and then give them plenty of opportunity to evaluate one another's work.

When you begin using the workshop approach, have student readers look for only one or two specific kinds of problems at a time. Let your own reading of student assignments guide you as you decide what to ask students to look for while editing. For example, if your class seems to write without enough supporting details, instruct student readers to look for places in their classmates' writing where additional specific details could be added. If selecting the most appropriate word seems to be a common problem, have students give feedback about that on another day.

Another helpful technique is to display anonymous examples of students' work as transparencies on an overhead projector. Point out examples that display the specific qualities of writing you're looking for, as well as examples that need improvement. You can avoid defensiveness or embarrassment on students' part by using anonymous work from a different class for your examples.

3. Organization and structure help students build a good piece of writing.

Most students don't suffer from a shortage of ideas, but organizing their thoughts in "permanent" form on paper can be difficult for them. They may not be sure about how to start, what ideas to include and what order to put them in. Clearly structured assignments, with specific step-by-step instructions, help circumvent this problem.

Young writers need help putting ideas and images into a logical structure. Many of the activities in this book are actually prewriting activities. They are intended to help students define and organize their thoughts coherently. But students must not stop there. Once they've completed that first activity, creating a final product should come much more easily. Make sure they see the process through to the end, and complete a final product.

21st Century Writing's appendix includes a variety of rubrics for evaluating student work. Ordinarily, students should know how they will be evaluated before they begin their assignment. Allow them to see the score sheet that will be used to evaluate them ahead of time. These score sheets can be used by students to evaluate one another as well. Your school system or state may also have developed specific rubrics for evaluating student writing. Allow students to use these as well.

Students' final products should be polished and carefully crafted. As teachers, we shouldn't settle for less. If it's not up to standards, encourage them to make it better; and don't penalize them when they do—reward them. We encourage teachers to adopt the following rule: If a student is willing to make the effort to revise and improve a piece of writing, we will take the time to re-evaluate it.

4. Whenever possible, student writing should be "real," not just an exercise.

Writers write so that others will read what they've written. Students should write for a genuine purpose whenever possible. They should know that they're not just practicing their skills for some unspecified future time or writing just for a grade. They can write real letters and actually mail them. They can submit their stories and essays to student newspapers and literary magazines.

At the very least, students should know that their work will be read by others. Build some method of sharing students' final products into each assignment. Some assignments in this book end with an activity that uses the students' final products. For others, give students the opportunity to read their work aloud, or post it on a bulletin board. Publish collections of students' best work. If students know that their work will be read by others, their motivation to do their best is much higher. They'll get additional informal feedback from their audience, too.

Assignments need not be deadly serious in order to instruct. Poets, essayists and novelists find joy in the sounds and rhythms of words and in saying exactly what they mean, in precisely the right way. Student writers can experience some of that same pleasure. We hope the activities in this book are good-humored, entertaining and thought-provoking.

Take the time to present examples of good writing to your students. Read to them and with them. In the work of published authors, point out examples of the skills you have been trying to improve upon in class.

Let students know that you appreciate excellent writing. Take time to read a passage and discuss what makes it especially clear, interesting or beautiful. Point out the power of language to convince, intrigue, inform, entertain and move us. If you let students know that you are passionate about writing, that passion will be contagious.

Even the editing process can be fun. Student writers often say something in a way that can be taken differently than it was intended, sometimes to humorous effect. Being able to laugh at our own mistakes makes the writing process more relaxed and less threatening. Teachers, be prepared to accept corrections from the editors you create. When your students start editing your exercises, tests and board work, you'll know your instruction has taken root.

Should students be required to complete a final product for each writing project they start? Professional writers certainly don't. Sometimes professionals realize that one of their writing projects is just not worth the effort. Perhaps students could be required to produce a certain number of final products to be evaluated during each grading period. A student who creates longer, more complex pieces may be allowed to finish fewer. We want students to be fluent in their writing. But we also want to encourage elaboration and the effort to make their written language as beautiful and elegant as possible.

Of course, teachers can also enjoy the satisfaction of stating their ideas clearly and cleverly in writing. Participate along with your students in at least some of the activities in this book. You'll become powerful role models for your students to follow. Have fun, and enjoy *21st Century Writing*.

Revising and Rewriting
Teacher Instructions

A Good Writer CARES
(Student Exercises R-1 through R-8)

Teaching the CARES acronym will give students a structure to help them revise their work (Change, Add, Rearrange, Eliminate, Standardize). There is at least one exercise for each of the five processes. Exercise R-8 gives students the opportunity to apply all five actions as they create revision problems for classmates to solve.

You may want to make copies of the CARES poster to put on your bulletin board to remind students of the CARES processes.

Writers' Workshop
(Student Exercise R-9)

Give each student a copy of these guidelines before you have them exchange their writings with each other for feedback.

You may also want to give students practice giving feedback using some sample student work before they use their own writings in a workshop setting. Build a file of sample student work, with names blacked out, that your students can use for practice. Or team up with another teacher, and exchange anonymous copies of student work for each class to read and edit.

You may need to explain the ideas of voice and tone. *Voice* is the idea that a writer's work shows individuality—that the personality of the writer is reflected in his or her words. (This is a different meaning of the word *voice* from that found in exercise R-15.)

Tone means "the appropriate emotional content." If the writer is angry, or sad about something, that should show in the sound of his or her words. If the writer is trying to be humorous, the choice of words and rhythms of the sentences should suit that mood.

Revising: Vivid Verbs and Specific Nouns
(Student Exercises R-10 through R-13)

Using interesting, precise nouns and verbs is the best way to create lively, descriptive writing. Writing that relies too heavily on adjectives and adverbs for description sounds unnatural and forced.

Use these exercises if your students' writing uses ordinary, vague, anemic nouns and verbs instead of more interesting, specific, precise ones.

Revising: Show, Don't Tell
(Student Exercise R-14)

Instead of just telling about what's happening in a story, students can make their writing livelier and more interesting by using specific details to show readers what's going on. Writing that *shows* rather than *tells* involves the reader more effectively. This exercise provides examples and practice for students who need to use specific information to show the reader what they mean.

Revising: Using the Active Voice
(Student Exercises R-15A through R-15B)

A sentence is written in passive voice if the subject is the recipient of the action (The test was taken by John). In the active voice, the subject of the sentence is doing the action (John took the test). In most cases, when writers use the active voice, their writing is stronger. Use this exercise if your students are overusing the passive voice in their writing.

Revising: Stretch It—Elaborate with Details
(Student Exercise R-16)

Insufficient elaboration with supporting detail is one of the most common problems in student writing. This exercise provides practice if your students' writings lack specific details.

Using Direct Quotations

This page provides instructions on how to format quotations, something that is difficult for many students.

Make Your Final Draft Look Great!
(A Sample First Page)

Use this sample page to show students how to format their final drafts. You may want to turn this page into a slide for an overhead projector, or enlarge it and post it on a bulletin board.

Proofreading and Editing Practice
(Student Exercises R-17 and R-18)
Revising and Rewriting Practice
(Student Exercises R-19 through R-21)

The first two of these exercises present pieces of writing with numerous spelling, punctuation and grammatical errors. The students' task is to proofread, find the errors and correct them.

The remaining exercises are more challenging. Students will have to use all the CARES processes as they improve the writing. Students will probably disagree about some suggested changes. Use this as an opportunity to discuss which version makes for better writing. Remember, in many cases there will not be one "right" answer. What makes for good writing is sometimes a matter of personal taste. Student editors will probably disagree about these assignments, and that should create some interesting and useful discussions.

Revising and Rewriting
Le Mot Juste
(Student Exercises R-22 through R-24)

Each item presents three different versions of the same quotation. One is the original, and the others are not as good, for various reasons.

Individually, have students choose the version that they think is best for each item. Then discuss their answers as a class. Don't tell them the answer ahead of time! For each item, have students "vote" for their choices: a, b or c. Then ask students to explain and defend their choices. Finally, tell them which version is the original quotation.

A Good Writer CARES

C hange—a word to a clearer, more precise word.

A dd—new ideas and details.

R earrange—the order of words, sentences or paragraphs.

E liminate—unnecessary words or ideas.

S tandardize—spelling, grammar and punctuation.

Name _______________________

A Good Writer CARES

No writing is finished after one draft. To make it great, you have to revise it. Revising is not just checking spelling and recopying. You have to find every place where you can make your writing better, and change what you've written. Professional writers revise over and over again. Every word must be exactly right before a writer decides a story, poem or article is finished.

If you are going to do your best writing, you'll have to revise, too. Before you turn in an assignment, read over what you've written. Make improvements. It's the ONLY way to write something that is truly your best work.

Here's an easy guide to help you remember what to do when you revise. Just remember the word CARES. Every good writer CARES for his or her writing.

CARES stands for:
    Change—a word you've written to a clearer, more precise word
    Add—new ideas and details
    Rearrange—the order of your words, sentences or paragraphs
    Eliminate—unnecessary words or ideas
    Standardize—spelling, grammar and punctuation

Here is an example of each step.

Change: Sue ~~laughed~~ giggled when the ~~dog's~~ puppy's tail touched her cheek.

Add: The puppy was (tiny and) brown. (He had big, friendly eyes.)

Rearrange: ~~Sue had never seen such a cuddly, cute dog in all her life.~~
He was the cutest, cuddliest dog she had ever seen.

Eliminate: She wanted the dog more than anything else in the world ~~she'd ever wanted~~.

Standardize: Please ~~lets~~ let's take him home, " Sue ~~beged~~ begged.

When a writer CARES, it makes a big difference. Your writing will be better!

- Fold the top of your paper down to this line.- -

Can you remember what the letters in CARE stand for? Let's see. Remember, each one is something you should do when you revise your writing.

C stands for _______________________________________

A stands for _______________________________________

R stands for _______________________________________

E stands for _______________________________________

S stands for _______________________________________

Student Exercise R-2

A Good Writer CARES

The C in CARES stands for CHANGE.

There can be many different ways to say any one idea. A good writer tries to find the best way. For example, suppose a character in your story looked out a window. You might want to change that word to *stared, peeked, peered, glared* or *glanced*. It would all depend on what was happening in the story. Each word would give your story a slightly different meaning, so it's important to choose just the right one.

After you've written your first draft, read it over carefully. Look for words or phrases that should be changed—changed to make your writing more interesting, or to say what you mean more exactly.

Let's practice changing some words. In each sentence below, change the word(s) in bold to make the sentence more precise and exciting.

1. Bob **ran** up the path to his house.

2. "I never want to see you again," Jill **said**.

3. The **animal** howled at the moon.

4. "Aren't you finished yet?" David **said**.

5. Mr. Edwards turned his car onto the **road**.

6. **I don't like** your new haircut.

7. The tiger **moved** through the jungle.

8. It was the strangest **thing** my family had ever seen.

9. That certainly is a **big** box.

10. **"Wow,"** Cynthia shouted.

For these sentences, find one or more words that you want to change. Make each sentence more interesting, more specific or more descriptive.

1. The fire began to burn out of control. ____

2. "I don't believe you one bit," Nancy said. ____

3. Mr. White came into the room with an interesting machine. ____

4. The tall, strong athlete ran around the track. ____

5. She heard a scary sound that came from somewhere in the dark woods. ____

____

Student Exercise R-3

A Good Writer CARES

The A in CARES means ADD. Sometimes you may leave important ideas out of your first draft. Sometimes you leave out small details that would make your writing more interesting. Look for places where you can ADD to what you've written. You might ADD just a word or two. You may ADD a whole sentence—or even more.

Remember, people can't read your mind. If you want them to know what you're thinking, tell them. You have to write it down! So check your writing for places where you've left something out—places to ADD something that makes your ideas clearer.

Make each of the sentences below more interesting by adding at least one more word or phrase.

1. Walter slammed the door and ran to his room.

2. Mrs. Fowler opened her shop at 10 o'clock on Saturday.

3. The craft landed on the lawn.

4. Dennis knew that he was in trouble.

5. Snow covered all the houses and trees.

6. The classroom was noisy and messy.

7. It had been raining all day long.

8. Keisha answered the telephone.

9. The children spent all afternoon playing.

10. Mr. Jefferson's office was on the 15th floor.

Student Exercise R-4

A Good Writer CARES

Here's a simple story that needs more details. ADD a new sentence between each sentence to make the story better.

Jane wanted a dog. ____

____

One day she looked outside and saw a puppy. _______________________

____

The puppy was lost. _______________________________________

____

Jane went outside and made friends with the dog._____________________

____

She took it inside and fed it. ________________________________

____

Her mother asked where the dog came from. _________________________

____

Jane told her. ____

____

Jane's mother said she could keep the little dog. ____________________

____

Jane was very happy. ______________________________________

____

Name _______________________________

A Good Writer CARES

The R in CARES means REARRANGE. The order of words in a sentence is important. Look at these two sentences, for example:

> Driving down the highway, Laura saw a moose.
> Laura saw a moose driving down the highway.

Both sentences have exactly the same words. But they are arranged differently, so they have different meanings.

Some sentences sound stronger if you rearrange them.

> The heavy container was lifted by the burly man.
> The burly man lifted the heavy container.

Most people would say that the second sentence is much better, because the person doing the action is used as the subject of the sentence.

The order of ideas and events is important, too. Many stories are told in the order that the events happen. Here's a short example that's out of order.

> The masked man quietly pushed the door open. He turned the doorknob slowly, so it wouldn't make a sound.

And here's the same sentences, REARRANGED so the events are in order.

> The masked man turned the doorknob slowly, so it wouldn't make a sound. Then he quietly pushed the door open.

Rearrange the following sentences and short paragraphs to make them sound better or make more sense.

1. With a crashing sound, Jim heard the bowling ball hit the pins.

2. The thief died, and he was shot by the bank guard.

3. How would you let someone know you have a problem? Knowing how to write letters is important. Suppose you had a complaint about a product you bought.   And a letter lets you keep a record of your complaint. A letter to the company that made the product usually gets quick action.

4. On the grill, Mr. Jackson cooked a thick, juicy steak.

5. The trapper lit the pile of firewood. Gathering the wood was hard work. It was very cold. Without a fire, the trapper knew he might freeze. His hands were stiff and painful. Finally he had collected enough for a campfire.

6. The nurse put a bandage on his finger, pulled the splinter out and swabbed it with alcohol.

7. Mrs. Wilson had a good day. She got a raise at work, won a million dollars in the state lottery, visited with an old friend and heard her favorite song on the radio.

8. The letter was 10 minutes late. It was delivered by a messenger at eleven thirty.

Student Exercise R-6

A Good Writer CARES

Sometimes a first draft has words, or even whole sentences, that aren't needed. They don't add anything to what you've written. Maybe you've repeated yourself, or maybe you've written something that doesn't belong with the rest of your story or poem. Don't try to make your work better by using big fancy words or unnecessarily complex sentences. Good writing is simple, clear and direct. When you revise your work, ELIMINATE unnecessary words and ideas. For example:

Charlie was ~~really,~~ really angry. He had never been treated so badly before. ~~He was mad.~~ How could they have done this to him?

Read the sentences below. Eliminate unnecessary words and phrases. You may also have to rearrange the sentence to make it sound better.

1. I want each and every one of you to open your books to page 35 in your textbooks.

2. The tired old Siamese cat, who was very old, curled up on the carpet and purred softly.

3. Marshall was afraid that the test would be very difficult and challenging, but it turned out that it was both easy and simple.

4. The breezy wind whistled through the trees, making a whooshing sound.

5. One half of the room was painted the color blue, and the other half of the room was painted the color white.

In each paragraph below, find an unnecessary sentence that can be eliminated.

6. Walter needed to build a doghouse. His dog, Busby, was getting too big to sleep inside. Walter's cat slept underneath the kitchen table. When Busby jumped up on the bed, Walter could feel the springs getting ready to give way. And when he started growling in his sleep in the middle of the night, Busby woke up the entire family.

7. Matson opened his briefcase and looked inside. It was empty! The briefcase was made of the finest leather. The handcuff that linked his wrist to the handle of the case was still locked securely. It hadn't been out of his sight all day, but somehow, the papers had been removed!

8. Mrs. Jasper studied her garden proudly. Everything was growing beautifully. The corn stalks were already six feet tall, and she could see the orange tops of carrots peeking out of the ground. Carrots are a good source of vitamin A. The first tomatoes were beginning to turn red, and the cabbages were just about ready to pick. Yes, it looked like it would be a good harvest.

Name ______________________________

A Good Writer CARES

The S in CARES stands for Standardize. Your first draft probably has spelling, grammar and punctuation errors. When you revise, one of your jobs is to find those mistakes and fix them so your work follows the rules of standard English. Papers without mistakes show that you're proud of your work, and that you've worked hard to make it as perfect as possible.

Remember, a computer spell checker won't catch all your mistakes! To a computer, *there, their* and *they're* are all spelled correctly.

If you're not sure whether something you have written is in standard form, you may be able to find an answer in a grammar book or style guide.

Read the sentences below. Eliminate spelling, punctuation and grammatical errors.

1. "I used to think I would never like to ate fish the old sailer said."

2. After church Wilson brought the twins home to meat his mother and grandfarther.

3. "My brother never makes misteaks." Bennie bosted. "Hes perfect."

4. Ralph drew a picture of a anteloupe running, across a grassy plane.

5. "Did you see this mornings newspaper," Mrs. Bolton asked? "The Mayor has resigned!"

6. All the jewlry was locked safely in the closet or so they thought.

7. Both boys we're sent to the principle's office.

8. Can sunspots effect radio reception hear on Earth?

9. Be careful you don't want to loose that beautiful ring!

10. We could of finished the project if we'd had just a few more minuets.

Student Exercise R-8

A Good Writer CARES
Do-It-Yourself CARES Exercise

Now that you know how a writer CARES, you should be able to make a worksheet for someone else to answer.
Write some sentences that need improvements. Then someone else in your class will have to fix them.

1. Write a sentence with a word or words that could be CHANGED to make the sentence better.

____

2. Now write another one.

____

3. Write a sentence which needs some words or ideas ADDED to it.

____

4. Write another.

____

5. Write a sentence which needs to be REARRANGED.

____

6. And a second one.

____

7. Write a sentence which has unnecessary words that should be ELIMINATED.

____

8. Write one more.

____

9. Write a sentence with grammar, spelling or punctuation errors that need to be STANDARDIZED.

____

10. And write one more.

____

Exchange papers with a classmate, and revise each other's sentences.

Name _______________________________

Writers' Workshop
Helping One Another Become Better Writers

Writing class will often be taught as a workshop. That means you'll share your work with other students. Your classmates will suggest ways to improve what you have written, and you'll make suggestions to help them.

Here are some questions to ask your classmates when you exchange writings. You shouldn't ask them all. Concentrate on areas you want to improve. You choose what feedback to ask for from your readers.

What do you think my main idea is?

Are there places where you were confused?

Did I include enough details? Do my words paint a picture in your mind?

Did I explain the reasons for my opinions?

What do you think I should add? Are there places where you need more information?

What do you think I should eliminate?

Does my organization make sense? What should I rearrange?

Voice: Does my writing sound like me? Is it written in my voice? What makes it sound like my voice, or not like my voice?

Tone: Does the writing sound like I mean what I'm saying? Does it show the appropriate emotion for the topic? If not, how could I change it?

Did my opening sentences get you interested?

Does the writing have a strong ending?

What do you think is the strongest part? The weakest part? Why?

Ask your readers for details and explanations about their comments. And remember, you can decide whether or not to take any suggestions you are given. After all, you are the author.

Adapted from the Virginia SOL Writing Tests: *A Teacher's Resource Notebook, Virginia. Department of Education.*

Student Exercise R-10

Revising: Vivid Verbs

Good writing describes events precisely and makes the reader see or feel events by using precisely the right verbs. For example, look at these sentences:

Mrs. Johnston **walked** across the street.
Mrs. Johnston **stormed** across the street.
Mrs. Johnston **crept** across the street.
Mrs. Johnston **rushed** across the street.
Mrs. Johnston **ambled** across the street

In each sentence the same thing happened: Mrs. Johnston crossed the street. But in each one, the verbs tell a completely different story.

There is probably no better way to make your writing interesting than to use lively, interesting verbs that say exactly what you want to say.

Here's your chance! Rewrite each of the following sentences three times, using three very different verbs.

1. James ate the sandwich. ____

2. The dog jumped over the hedge. _______________________________________

3. The jet lifted off the runway. ____

4. Stacy ran around the track.____

5. Grandpa got out of bed. ____

6. The boy took the cookie. ____

7. "Let me in," Ashley said. ____

8. Walter hit his friend. ____

Finally, write a paragraph that tells about something you did this morning. It could be about getting dressed, making breakfast, riding the bus or talking with your friends. As you write, tell what happened using specific, vivid verbs.

____

____

____

Student Exercise R-11

Revising: Vivid Verbs

Adverbs help describe the action of a verb. Adverbs can make an action more vivid and precise, but there is often a better way to create interesting sentences. A strong verb builds a better sentence than a weak verb modified by an adverb.

Each sentence below has a bold verb and modifying adverb(s). Rewrite each sentence twice, using stronger, more vivid verbs.

Example:

"I'm tired of waiting in this line," Andrew <u>said angrily</u>.

"I'm tired of waiting in this line," Andrew fumed.   "I'm tired of waiting in this line," Andrew grumbled.

1. Carlos **walked cautiously** across the muddy field.

____

2. "Please let me go with you," Kristen **asked pleadingly**.

____

3. Susan **spoke loudly** to her friend across the room.

____

4. The squirrel **walked nimbly** along the telephone line.

____

5. "I don't want any!" José **said angrily**.

____

6. Amy **looked** at the photographs **closely**.

____

7. Michael **ran swiftly** around the track.

____

8. Annette **did** her work **sloppily** in her notebook.

____

9. The sentry **looked cautiously** at the enemy lines.

____

10. Mrs. Williams **put** the groceries on the table **carelessly**.

____

Name _______________________________

Revising: Specific Nouns

Good writing describes events precisely, by using just the right nouns. For example, look at these sentences:

The **woman** walked across the street.
Ms. Johnston walked across the street.
The **bride** walked across the street.
The **actress** walked across the street.

In each sentence an adult female crossed the street. All four sentences could be about the same person. But each sentence gives us different information about her. To say exactly what you want to say, use nouns that are carefully chosen to identify people and things precisely.

Rewrite each of the following sentences three times. Replace the underlined word or words with three different, specific nouns. You may use names, but no more than one for each item in the exercise.

1. Charlene drank the <u>drink</u>._______________________________

   ____

2. The <u>dog</u> snarled at his owner. _______________________________

   ____

3. The <u>car</u> rounded the corner. _______________________________

   ____

4. The <u>boy</u> caught the ball._______________________________

   ____

5. The man cooked <u>some food</u>. _______________________________

   ____

6. William read the <u>words</u>. _______________________________

   ____

7. Danielle shouted at the <u>girl</u>. _______________________________

   ____

8. The <u>house</u> was damaged in the fire._______________________________

   ____

Finally, write a paragraph that describes your kitchen counter or your kitchen table. First picture it clearly in your mind. Then, as you write, describe your subject with specific, precise nouns.

Student Exercise R-13

Revising: Vivid Verbs and Specific Nouns

Rewrite each sentence to make it more interesting by using more specific nouns, adjectives and vivid verbs.

1. The animal ran across the field.

   ____

2. The man spoke to the child.

   ____

3. An object hit the building.

   ____

4. The paper told him about the event.

   ____

5. A boy moved the furniture.

   ____

6. A vessel moved across the water.

   ____

7. The girl got the book.

   ____

8. A bird looked for food.

   ____

9. This machine cuts things.

   ____

10. A plant grew near the building.

    ____

11. The teacher talked to the student.

    ____

12. The vehicle moved down the road.

    ____

Student Exercise R-14

Revising: Show, Don't Tell

You've probably heard the expression "actions speak louder than words." It's certainly true in writing. Whenever possible, show your readers what you mean, rather than telling them.

For example, you could *tell* us: Julie was very angry.
Or, you could *show* us instead: Julie threw the notebook on the floor and stormed out the door, slamming it hard enough to rattle the glasses on the kitchen table.

You could *tell* us: The woods were dark and scary.
Or, you could *show* us: We could barely see the outline of the trees beside the path. We stepped slowly, hands out in front of us. Spiderwebs clung to our faces. Above us was a fluttering of unseen wings and the faint scratching of claws on bark.

When you write a story or essay, try to show the reader what's going on, rather than just telling about it. It makes your writing much more interesting to read. It gives the reader more opportunity to participate in the story, to think about the events and make inferences about why they are taking place.

Here are several sentences. Each *tells* about something in a story. Revise any six of them, using specific details, so that they *show* what's happening instead of telling.

1. Jason had never felt happier. ____

2. The appearance of the sky and the ocean warned of the coming storm. __________________

____

3. Maria couldn't decide which instrument to choose. _______________________________

4. The rain forest was lush and damp and full of life. _______________________________

5. Denise was very worried about the test. _______________________________________

6. The weightlifter was amazingly strong. _______________________________________

7. The old house was badly in need of repair. _____________________________________

8. The dolphin was both fast and graceful as it swam. _______________________________

9. It was a very hot day. ____

10. The intersection was very busy during rush hour. ________________________________

Student Exercise R-15A

Revising: Using the Active Voice

One way to make your writing stronger is to use the active voice. When you write in the active voice, the person or thing doing the action is the subject of your sentence. In passive voice, the subject of the sentence has the action happening to it.

Active Voice: Mr. Martinez ate the sandwich
Passive Voice The sandwich was eaten by Mr. Martinez.
Active Voice: The wolves chased the deer across the frozen tundra.
Passive Voice The deer were chased across the frozen tundra by the wolves.

Here are some sentences. Mark them AV if they use the active voice. Mark them PV if they use the passive voice.

________ 1. The gift was given by the whole class to Mrs. MacArthur.

________ 2. Addy's joke made everyone giggle.

________ 3. Allison fainted when Mr. Wynn cut into the starfish.

________ 4. Jack's accident was caused by his little brother.

________ 5. Johnny's furniture was moved by his sister and her friend.

________ 6. The dog was hit by the delivery truck.

________ 7. Ms. Armstead made Durrell spit his gum into the trashcan.

________ 8. The grizzly caught the salmon on the first try.

________ 9. The guests were called to dinner by the butler.

________ 10. Our teacher retired after 40 years of work in the same school building.

Student Exercise R-15B

Revising: Using the Active Voice

Make your writing stronger by using active voice instead of passive voice. Remember, in passive voice, the subject of the sentence has the action happening to it. When you write a sentence in the active voice, the person or thing doing the action is the subject.

Passive Voice   The fort on the hillside was captured by the soldiers.
Active Voice: The soldiers captured the fort on the hillside.

Passive voice sounds weak. It's almost always better to write sentences so that the actor is the subject. It makes your writing stronger and more direct.

Sometimes a sentence in passive voice doesn't even name the person or thing doing the acting.

For example: A paper airplane was tossed across the room.

To change this to the active voice, you must name the person who tossed the plane:
Henry tossed a paper airplane across the room.

Or, make the airplane the subject of the sentence: The paper airplane floated across the room.

Some of the sentences below are written in the passive voice. If a sentence is written in passive voice, rewrite it so that it is in the active voice. Don't rewrite sentences that are already written in the active voice.

1. After lunch, a nap was taken by all the children. ________________________________

2. Eloise ate three helpings of mashed potatoes. ________________________________

3. The new computer was turned on by the technician. ________________________________

4. Five beautifully wrapped boxes were placed under the tree. ________________________________

5. My brother's gerbil ran up Mr. Winston's leg. ________________________________

6. The game was played by everyone in the room. ________________________________

7. The moon slipped behind a cloud. ________________________________

8. The fish would soon be caught by the eagle circling overhead. ________________________________

9. Piece by piece, the engine was reassembled. ________________________________

10. Our bus driver looked at the map before he drove away. ________________________________

Student Exercise R-16

Revising: Stretch It— Elaborate with Details

A common problem with some student writing is that it doesn't have enough detail. Specific details are very important in any piece of writing.

• Details provide support for your ideas.
• Details make any piece of writing more interesting to read.
• Details can make your writing seem more realistic.

When you revise a first draft of a story or essay, you can often improve it by adding more specific details. If your writing is usually short on details, skip lines as you write a first draft. This strategy will make it easier to add details later.

Of course, more isn't always better. Details should add some useful information to your writing, rather than interrupting the flow of ideas.

Below is a simple essay. Add specific details to make it more interesting to read. First, make notes in the space between the lines. Then, rewrite your improved version of the essay on a piece of notebook paper.

Over the past 20 years, computers have become part of our everyday lives. We use them at work. We use

them at school. We use computer chips to control complicated machinery. It's hard to imagine any modern

business running successfully without computers to communicate with customers, keep records and conduct

financial transactions. In our homes, computers are everywhere. They are embedded in our appliances. We

rely on them to communicate with other people. And we use them to keep ourselves entertained. It's hard to

imagine how our lives would change if all our computers were suddenly taken away.

Quotations can make a piece of writing come alive. Let your readers hear what the people you are writing about have to say. Their words will show what they think and what their personalities are like.

When you quote people in your writing, there are certain rules to follow:

• Write a speaker's words inside quotation marks. Capitalize the first word of each sentence the speaker says. Only the speaker's exact words go inside the quotation marks.

• Use a comma or other punctuation mark between the speaker's words and the words that identify the speaker. ("Let's go," Bob said.) If a speaker says several sentences, enclose them all within a single set of quotation marks. ("Let's go! We're already late," Bob said.) Notice that punctuation marks go inside the quotation marks.

• Start a new paragraph for each new speaker, even if that person speaks only a single word.

• If the speaker asks a question or makes an exclamation, the question mark or exclamation mark goes inside the quotation mark. ("Are you ready?" Bob asked.) You still need a period at the end of the sentence.

• Make sure your reader knows who is speaking. If you're writing a conversation between two people, you need not identify the speaker every single time. But you must do it often enough to make it clear who is speaking each line.

• Longer quotations of more than one paragraph are formatted differently. Put quotation marks at the beginning of each paragraph, but put the closing quotation marks only at the very end of the entire quotation.

• When you use a long quotation (four lines or more) in a report or research paper, indent the entire quotation on both the left and right margins. Don't use any quotation marks at all. At the end of the quotation, indicate the source of the words. A long quotation in a report should look like this:

> The amount of available nitrogen, potassium and phosphorus limit how much life a region of the ocean can support. Coastal waters like the Chesapeake Bay are greenish in color because the rich supply of nutrients helps algae grow. On the other hand, the beautiful blue waters around many tropical islands are clear because there are so few nutrients to support the growth of algae. (Fleisher, Our Oceans, page 17)

A Sample First Page

Make Your Final Draft Look Great!

Arthur Wright
English 7-A, Period 4
November 12, 2003

A well-formatted product shows that you are a capable, experienced writer. If your paper is sloppy, careless or too fancy, readers will take your work less seriously.

What should a final draft look like? It should look like this page. It should be typed or printed in black ink. Double-space, using 12-point type. Leave two spaces after each period and one space after each comma. Indent each paragraph about a half an inch from the left margin.

Avoid fancy typefaces that are difficult to read. Choose a typeface with serifs (little tails on the letters). They are easier to read than typefaces without them. Don't use graphics, unless they add supporting information to your words.

Print your final draft on plain white paper, with one-inch margins. If you use a word processor, type, edit and proofread your work first. Save the formatting of your paper for last. If you are turning in a handwritten paper, write in black or blue pen. Use your neatest handwriting, and write on only one side of the paper.

At the top of the first page, place a heading with your name and the other information your teacher requires. Skip two lines, and center your title. Skip two more lines, and begin the story or essay. Put your name at the top of each succeeding page, too.

Title pages or blank cover sheets are unnecessary. Unless your teacher requests them, don't use plastic report covers. They make papers slippery and hard to handle.

Proofreading and Editing Practice 1

Find all the errors in spelling, grammar and punctuation in the following excerpt from an essay. Circle and correct each error.

The rain forest of Costa Rico is lush and humid, tall trees shade the forest floor. Smaller plants and vines reach upward to gather as mush sunlight as it can.

In the forest canopy, a brightly-colored toucan searches for nuts to crack in its powerful beek. Meanwhile, a fury brown agouti—a large rodent—feeds on fruits and berries that have fallen from the canopy to the sparse under growth below.

Nearby, a group of howler monkeys swing through the trees. The monkeys use their long tales to hold firmly to a branch as they reach out for the tastest young leaves to eat. The silverback male threats us with loud growls if we get to near.

A red and blue frog hops along the rotting wood of an algae-covered tree limb. The bright colors are a warning. Stay away! The slimmy liquid that covers the skin of this little frog is very toxic? Native hunters once used these frogs to tip their arrows and darts with poison.

The rain forest is full of facsinating creatures. But one of the most interesting and important of all is very small. Thousands of leafcutter ants parade back and fourth acrost the damp forest floor in a never-ending stream, the ants carry bits of leaves harvested from a nearby tree. They look like they're carrying tinny umbrellas. Each peice of leaf is smaller then a dime. Where are they going. What will they do with all those leaves? The answer will amaze you.

Student Exercise R-18

Proofreading and Editing Practice 2

Find all the errors in spelling, grammar and punctuation in the following excerpt from an essay. Circle and correct each error.

Although they might not look like it, seahorse are fish. Like other fish, they have a skeliton, gills and small fins. Instead of scales, seahorses are covered with hard, boney plates.

Seahorses live in warm shallow waters. Where there is plenty of seaweed or sea grasses. They cling to the underwater plants with their flexable tails. Many seahorses change color to blend into their surroundings. This camouflage protects them from predators, and hides them as they wait among the plants, for their prey. When small animals swims by, a seahorse snaps their jaws open with a clicking sound and suck the prey into their mouths.

Seahorses are beautiful creatures But what's most special about them is their unusaul life cycle. Seahorse males give birth? Adult males have a pouch below their belly where baby seahorses develop and grow.

The female places 150-200 eggs into the males pouch with a tube called an ovipositor . The female's part in raising the young is then finished. The male fertilizes the eggs inside his pouch.

The female visits the male each day. They greet each other by changing colors, linking tails and swimming together! Then the female goes off to feed.

Finally, after sevaral weeks the male seahorse, pushes the babies out of her pouch. He releases the babies in groups over several days. Sometimes he push against rocks or other hard objects to squeeze the baby's out.

Baby seahorses look like miniature versions of their parents. The babies hide from predators in the sea grass. for a few days they swim in a horizontal position like other fish. Then they switch to an upright position, like their parents.

Student Exercise R-19

Revising and Rewriting Practice 1

The following story excerpt needs editing. Change words to be more vivid and specific. Add details. Rearrange sentences that are out of order. Eliminate unnecessary words and ideas, and standardize all errors in spelling, grammar and punctuation.

Island Formation

Islands form in a number of different ways. Many islands are volcanic in origin. Undersea volcanos pour out huge amounts of larva, forming undersea mountains that may eventually rise above the surface of the ocean. The Hawaiian Islands and Iceland are both two examples of islands that formed in this way.

Other islands are formed by the growth of coral. Corals are small animals related to jellyfish. They have stinging tenticles that they use to capture pray from the waters around them. Unlike jellyfish, corals live in huge colonies attached to a solid surface. They must live in shallow water, because each animal has special algae—called zooxanthellae—that grow inside it. The algae need sunlight to grow. Zooxanthellae produce much of the food that corals need to survive.

Each coral animal builds a small limestone cups in which it lives. When it dies, the limestone is left behind! Other corals grow on top of it. Over many years, corals build up great reefs. If sea level drops, these reefs are exposed, they become limestone islands. The Bahamas and the Florida keys were created in this way.

Other islands are produced as wind and waves pile up mounds of sand in coastal shallow waters. These barrier islands start as underwater sandbars that waves create in shallow offshore waters. The Island gathers more and more sand carried by the wind and waves. Gradually, the waves may build the sandbar into a new island. Grasses and other plants take root. The plants help hold the sand in place, and create windbreaks that capture even more sand. Changes in sea level and great storms can also expose or drown barrier islands. Miami beach, the Outer Banks in North Carolina and Atlantic City, New jersey are all barrier islands.

35

Student Exercise R-20

Revising and Rewriting Practice 2

The following story excerpt needs editing. Change words to be more vivid and specific. Add details. Rearrange sentences that are out of order. Eliminate unnecessary words and ideas, and standardize all the errors in spelling, grammar and punctuation.

An oyster spends its adult life firmly attached to a solid surface like a rock or a shell. It never moves. But an oyster don't start its life attached to a rock or shell. In it's growth from egg to adult, this animal goes through many different changes.

An oyster begins life as a tiny fertilized egg floating in the warm waters of a bay or inlet. After about 10 hours, the egg hatches into a tiny little larva. No bigger than a speck of dust. The larva has a fringe of tiny hair-like cilia that it uses to row itself through the water. The cilia also filter tiny food partacles out of the water for the larva to eat.

After just one day, the larva change form. It now looks like a tiny swimming clam. Dozens of these larvae could fit on the head of a pin. Each larva has a thin shell and a little foot, much like a clam. It also has many cilia. It floats and swims along with the water currents, straining particles of food from the water with its cilia.

The oyster larvae float and swim in the warm waters, eating and growing. Most of the larvae end up as food for other animals that live in the bay. Oysters are one of the most popular items in seafood restaurants.

After about two weeks, each surviving larva sinks to the bottom of the bay. It searches for a hard surface to attach itself—a rock, concreate, a piece of wood or even another oyster shell. The larva then attaches its shell to the surface of the rock, concrete, wood or shell and never moves again. The young oyster begins growing the heavy shell that will be its home for the rest of its life.

By the end of its first year, the young oyster will be about an inch long. Oysters begin reprodusing when they are about a year old. Oysters spawn in late spring. When the water temperature reaches about 68 degrees F. If the water gets warmer than 85 degrees F, spawning ends.

All young adult oysters are male. During the summer mating season, they release billions of sperm into the water to fertilize the eggs of other oysters. But after their first year, something surprising happens, young male oysters turn into older female oysters. Once an oyster has changed from male to female, it remains female for the rest of its life.

Female oysters produce enormouse numbers of eggs. The average oyster produces 15 million eggs or more in a single summer! Very few of these eggs survive to become adults, though. Most become food for other creatures in the bay? An adult oyster can live for six years or more.

The female oysters release her eggs into the water. When a female spawns, it opens and closes its shells, pumping out millions of eggs in about twenty minutes. Oysters produce chemical signals that signal other oysters to begin spawning also. However many different oysters release their sperm and egg cells into the water at the same time. This makes it more likely that eggs and sperm cells will meet in the water. The eggs develop into tiny oyster larvae, starting the life cycle all over again.

Student Exercise R-21

Revising and Rewriting Practice 3

The following story excerpt needs editing. Change words to be more vivid and specific. Add details.
Rearrange sentences that are out of order. Eliminate unnecessary words and ideas, and standardize all the
errors in spelling, grammar and punctuation.

The Tinker Case

Do students have the right to express ideas and opinions freely in School? Do they have the same First
Amendment protections as older Americans. In 1969, the supreme Court of the United States answered that
question when it ruled on the case of a young Iowa student. Their answer, which applies to every student in
the United States, was yes.

Mary Beth Tinker was 13 years old in 1965, when she decided to protest against U.S. involvement in
the war in Vietnam. Mary Beth, her fifteen-year-old brother John, and Christopher Eckhardt decided to speak
silently out against the war by wearing black armbands to school.

The school administration heard about there plans ahead of time and announced that anyone wearing
arm bands would be told to take it off. If they refused, they would be suspended. On the day of the protest,
that is exactly what happened. Mary Beth and the others wore their armbands, were sent home and were told
to remove them.

The school administrators claimed they had the right to prevent the wearing of arm bands and other
actions that might disrupt school discipline. But the three kids believed they had had the right to express their
opinions in school. With the support of their parents, they sued the Des Moines school system.

At their first trial, the judge agreed with the Des Moines School District. The students appealed.The
appeals court upheld the school administration. The student had one appeal left-to the U. S. Supreme Court.
The Supreme Court heard the case and decided in the student's favor by a vote of 7 to 2. The U.S. Supreme
court has nine members, and meets in Washington, D.C.

The opinion of the court was written by Justice Abe Fortas. In it he said students are guarantied the
same constitutional rights as everyone else. "It can hardly be argued that either students or teachers shed their
constitutional rights to freedom of speech at the schoolhouse gate, the decision stated." The Supreme Court's
ruling ruled that education in a democracy must be democratic.

The case is officially called Tinker v. Des Moines Independent School District, although it is usually
just known to as the Tinker case. The Tinker case was a turning point in U.S. law. Dozens of other court
cases used the Tinker decision as the basis for protecting the rights of other students, as well as teachers. And
it all started with a couple of young students who had the courage to stand up for the right to express their
beliefs.

Student Exercise R-22

Revising and Rewriting: Le mot juste

Le mot juste. It's French for "Just the right word."

In this exercise, use everything you've learned about revising and rewriting. One of the choices in each set is a famous quotation, in its original form. The others are poor imitations of the real thing. Decide which version is best. You will have to explain the reasons for your choice.

_________ 1.   a. My poems are songs to the lifes' glory.
           b. My poems are hymns of praise to the glory of life.
           c. My poetry sing the praises of the glory of life.

_________ 2.   a. It is better to know some of the questions than all of the answers.
           b. It is better to know some of the questions than the answers.
           c. Knowing some of the questions is better than the answers.

_________ 3.   a. I never forget a face, but in your case I'll make an exception.
           b. For you, I'll make an exception to my rule of never forgetting a face.
           c. I never forget a face, but in your case I'll be different.

_________ 4.   a. To be a leader of men, you must turn yourself around so that you are not facing them anymore.
           b. To be a leader of men, one must turn one's back on men.
           c. Turn your back on your men in order to be their leader of men.

_________ 5.   a. I can only offer except blood, toil, tears and sweat.
           b. I have nothing to give but blood and my toil and tears and my sweat.
           c. I have nothing to offer but blood, toil, tears and sweat.

_________ 6.   a. Don't be looking backwards. Somebody maybe gaining on you.
           b. Don't turn around while you're running. Some person or thing may be catching up to you.
           c. Don't look back. Something may be gaining on you.

_________ 7.   a. If you don't help solve the problem, you're not taking part in the solution.
           b. You're either part of the solution or part of the problem.
           c. Either you help solve the problem or you'll be seen as a cause of the problem.

Student Exercise R-23

Revising and Rewriting: Le mot juste 2

One of the choices in each set is a famous quotation. Decide which version is best. You will have to explain the reasons for your choice.

______ 1. a. Grownups never understand anything for themselves, and it is tiresome for children to be always and forever explaining things to them.
  b. Grownups never understand anything, and it is tiresome for a child always to be forever explaining things to him.
  c. A grownup never understands anything for himself, and they are tiresome when children must always and forever be explaining stuff to them.

____

______ 2. a. Man has wrested from nature the power to make the world a desert or to bloom the deserts.
  b. Man has wrested from nature the power to make the world a desert or the deserts bloom.
  c. Man has wrested from nature the power to make the world a desert or to make the deserts bloom.

____

______ 3. a. There is always one moment in childhood when the door opens and lets the future in.
  b. There is always one moment in childhood when the door opens and lets in the future.
  c. There is always one moment in childhood when the door opens and let's the future in.

____

______ 4. a. If an autonomous commonwealth cannot assist the many who are impoverished, it cannot safeguard the few who are affluent.
  b. If a free society cannot help the many who are broke, it cannot save the few who are loaded.
  c. If a free society cannot help the many who are poor, it cannot save the few who are rich.

____

______ 5. a. The sea lays all around us.
  b. The sea lies all around us.
  c. The seas lies all around us.

____

_______ 6.   a. The more things a man is ashamed of, the more respectable he is.
             b. The more things a man is ashamed of, the more respectable.
             c. The more things a man is ashamed of, the more respectable they are.

_______ 7.   a. When you have eliminated the impossible, whatever remains, however improbable, must be the truth.
             b. When you have eliminated the impossible, whatever remains, probable or not probable, must be the truth.
             c. When you have eliminated the impossible, what's left, however improbable, must be right.

_______ 8.   a. There is nothing wrong with our nation that cannot be fixed by what is right with America.
             b. There's nothing wrong with the U.S. of A. that can't be cured by what's right with us.
             c. There is nothing wrong with America that cannot be cured by what is right with America.

_______ 9.   a. Education is lighting of a fire, not filling of a pail.
             b. Education is not the filling of a pail, but the lighting of a fire.
             c. Education is not the filling of a pail but lighting a fire, instead.

_______ 10.   a. Restriction of free thought and speech is the dangerousmost of all subversions.
             b. Restriction of freedom of thought and free speech is the most dangerous subversions.
             c. Restriction of free thought and free speech is the most dangerous of all subversions.

40

Student Exercise R-24

Revising and Rewriting: Le mot juste 3

One of the choices in each set is a famous quotation. Decide which version is best. You will have to explain the reasons for your choice.

______ 1.
   a. The most stringent protection of free speech won't protect a man in falsely saying fire in a theatre and causing panic.
   b. The stringentmost protection of free speech would not protect a man in making a fake shout of fire in a theatre and causing a panic.
   c. The most stringent protection of free speech would not protect a man in falsely shouting fire in a theatre and causing a panic.

____

______ 2.
   a. Crime is contagious. If the government becomes a law-breaker, it breeds contempt for law.
   b. Crime is contagious. If the government was to become breaker of laws, it would breed contempt for law.
   c. Crime is contagious. If the government became a law-breaker, it is breeding contempt for law.

____

______ 3.
   a. We can have democracy in this country, and have great wealth concentrated in the hands of a few. But we can't have both.
   b. We can have democracy in this country, or we can have great wealth concentrated in the hands of a few, but we can't have both.
   c. We can have democracy in this country, or we can have great wealth concentrated in the hands of a few, so we can't have both.

____

______ 4.
   a. Contrasting to totalitarianism, democracy can face up and live with the truth about itself.
   b. In comparison with totalitarianism, democracy can face with and live with the truth about itself.
   c. In contrast to totalitarianism, democracy can face and live with the truth about itself.

____

______ 5.
   a. I believe in democracy because it releases the energy of every human being.
   b. I believe in democracy because it releases energy that everybody has.
   c. I believe in democracy because it frees the energy of each and every single individual man, woman and child.

____

_______ 6.
a. Man's capacity for justice makes democracy possible, but his inclination to injustice makes democracy necessary.
b. Man's capacity for justice makes democracy possible, but he is inclined towards injustice so it is necessary.
c. Man's capacity for justice makes it possible to have a democracy, but our inclination to injustice makes it necessary to govern ourselves that way.

_______ 7.
a. This will remain the land of the free only as long as it is the home of the courageous.
b. This will remain the land of the free only as long as it is the home of the brave.
c. This will remain the land of freedom only until it is no longer the home to the brave anymore.

_______ 8
a. It is a great thing to start life with a small number of really, really super books which are your very own.
b. It is a fantastically wonderful thing to start life with a small number of really good books which are your very own to keep for yourself.
c. It is a great thing to start life with a small number of really good books which are your very own.

_______ 9.
a. Despite all the things I've seen, I still think people are pretty okay.
b. I still believe in peoples' goodness, even though things look bad right now.
c. In spite of everything, I still believe that people are really good at heart.

_______ 10.
a. The two most powerful movers of the human mind are the desire for good, and being afraid of evil.
b. The two great movers of the human mind are the desire for good, and the fear of evil.
c. The two great movers of the human mind are being desirable of good, and the fear of evil.

Revising and Rewriting : Le mot juste, page 38

1. b. Dame Edith Sitwell
2. a. James Thurber
3. a. Groucho Marx
4. b. Havelock Ellis
5. c. Winston Churchhill
6. c. Satchel Paige
7. b. attributed to Eldridge Cleaver

Revising and Rewriting : Le mot juste 2, pages 39-40

1. a. Antoine de Saint-Exupery
2. c. Adlai E. Stevenson
3. a. Graham Greene
4. c. John F. Kennedy
5. b. Rachel L. Carson
6. a. George Bernard Shaw
7. a. Sir Arthur Conan Doyle
8. c. William Jefferson Clinton
9. b. William Butler Yeats
10. c. William O. Douglas

Revising and Rewriting: Le mot juste 3, pages 41-42

1. c. Oliver Wendell Holmes
2. a. Louis D. Brandeis
3. b. Louis D. Brandeis
4. c. Sydney Hook
5. a. Woodrow Wilson
6. a. Reinhold Niebuhr
7. b. Elmer Davis
8. c. Arthur Conan Doyle
9. c. Anne Frank
10. b. Samuel Johnson

Technical Writing

Teacher Instructions

Technical Writing
(Student Exercise T-1)

Can You Get There from Here?
(Student Exercise T-2)

You may want to introduce this activity by bringing in examples of poorly worded or confusing directions for use or assembly from various products. These poor examples will demonstrate how important clear technical writing is. Encourage students to search their own homes for additional examples to share with the class.

Make sure students have a copy of the score sheet (from the Appendix) before they begin their writing, so they know how they will be evaluated ahead of time.

When they have finished writing, ask several students to read their directions aloud. Specifically praise students who have written fully detailed instructions in a logical sequence. Make suggestions for improvement to those who have been insufficiently detailed, given instructions out of order or included unnecessary information. If possible, you may even send students into the hall to test their directions.

Use the Student Exercise T-2 to give students additional practice in writing precise, specific directions.

Additional Direction Writing Activity
(no student worksheet)

Have students write another set of directions. You may wish to give them several different choices:

a. Directions from their home to the school.
b. Directions from their home to the nearest public library.
c. Directions from school to the nearest public library.
d. Directions from school to City Hall.
e. Directions from home (or school) to their favorite shopping mall.
f. Directions from the mall parking lot to their favorite store.

After students have finished writing their directions, have them exchange with a partner. Partners should give feedback on whether the directions are clear and understandable, whether all the necessary information is included and whether extra, unnecessary information has been added.

Students should then revise and rewrite a final copy of their directions.

It's How You Play the Game
(Student Exercise T-3)

Instructions on the worksheet should be self-explanatory. Make sure students have the opportunity to exchange writings with a reader for feedback before they write their final product.

How to Make the Perfect Sandwich
(Student Exercise T-4)
How to . . . Cook an egg, etc. . . .
(Student Exercise T-5)

Allow students to use alternative topics if they suggest ones that seem suitable.

Again, have students exchange with a partner. Partners should give feedback on whether the directions are clear and understandable, whether all the necessary information is included and whether extra, unnecessary information has been added.

Students should then revise and rewrite a final copy of their directions.

Accessing Information on the Web
(Student Exercise T-6)

Give students copies of the exercise. If they are uncertain about the process of turning on the computer, starting up a web browser like Netscape Navigator and then doing a web search, take the time to review that with them.

Feel free to modify the topic of the search from poison ivy to something else.

If the classroom situation allows, give students an opportunity to check the accuracy of their directions on a computer.

Remind students that their final product should be written in paragraph form, using complete sentences. In evaluating their work, deduct points for work that does not meet that requirement.

Alien Instruction Manual
(Student Exercise T-7)

Complete instructions can be found on the reproducible student exercise.

How to Eat Your Words
(no student worksheet)

Gather enough materials: bread, peanut butter, jelly, paper plates, napkins and utensils ahead of time.

Have students write a set of detailed, precise instructions describing how to make a peanut butter and jelly sandwich.

Have them exchange with partners, get feedback and then write a final version of their instructions. Explain that they'll have to "eat their words."

Collect students' writings. Read each one aloud, and follow the directions literally, following whatever steps the student has described. Then present the resulting sandwich or mess to each student.

Note: depending on time and class size, you may have to limit your service to selected students.

Instructions for making other final products, such as cooking an egg, making toast with butter and jelly or making fresh lemonade can be substituted for the PB&J.

Map Directions
(Student Exercise T-8)
(no student worksheet)

Preparation: Obtain a number of United States or North American road maps. Make sure students know how to use the index to locate places on the map, and how to distinguish different kinds of roadways (state, national and interstate). This activity can also be done using state or local road maps.

1. Copy and cut apart the reproducible list of starting points and destinations. Divide students into groups of three to four, with a map for each group. Have each student draw a slip with a starting point and destination. Each student then writes a set of directions to instruct someone how to travel from one point to the other. Students then exchange their written directions with another group member, and check them to make sure they are accurate. Students give one another feedback.

2. Students draw a second starting point and destination. They should then write another set of directions—this time without mentioning the destination point by name. Again, have students exchange directions and follow them on the map, attempting to correctly identify the final destination.

3. Students should then choose a starting and ending point on the map, and write a third set of directions. Once again, exchange, have students follow the directions on the map and give feedback.

Student Exercise T-1

Technical Writing

Technical writing explains how to do something. The instruction manual for a computer game is an example of technical writing. So are the directions for putting together a model airplane, baking a cake from a mix or operating a nuclear power plant.

Good technical writing should be clear, precise, detailed and easy to follow. If the reader gets confused, he can't follow the directions. Then you get an inedible cake, or a nuclear meltdown.

Here's your first technical writing exercise:

Explain exactly how to get from your classroom to your principal's office. Be precise and detailed. Make sure you don't leave out anything. And no, you can't just write, "Break a school rule and get a referral."

Make sure you give your directions in order. Don't leave out any important details, and don't put in any information that is not needed to complete the task.

____

____

____

____

____

____

____

____

____

Once you are finished writing your directions, exchange with a classmate. Read each other's directions. Make sure nothing has been left out, and nothing extra has been added.

Give each other feedback. Then write a final copy of your directions.

Student Exercise T-2

Can You Get There from Here?

"... then walk about 50 feet, and take a left at the water cooler. You'll see a ...."

It's one thing to know where a particular place is. It's a lot harder to tell someone else how to get there! Let's see how well you can do it.

First, choose a location somewhere on the school grounds—either inside or outside the school building. Choose someplace fairly distant from your classroom. Write the place you've chosen here.

____

Now, without naming the place you've selected, write an exact set of directions that will tell someone how to get there from your classroom. Write your directions on the lines below. **LEAVE THE TOP LINE BLANK.**

After you've written your directions, tear your paper along the dotted line. Exchange your directions with a classmate. Read the directions and see if you can figure out what to write on the top line.

DIRECTIONS TO _________________________________

____

____

____

____

____

____

____

____

48

Student Exercise T-3

It's How You Play the Game
A Team Activity

Every game has specific rules about how it is to be played, what behaviors are allowed and what is not permitted. For this activity, choose a partner. Then choose a simple game you are both familiar with. Here are some suggestions: Hopscotch; Four Square; Rock, Paper, Scissors; Old Maid; marbles; jacks; arm wrestling; Go Fish.

Now, each of you should write a set of directions that explain how to play the game. Think about how you will organize your directions. You should probably start by explaining the object of the game. Make sure you include information about the number of players, how players take turns and what each player does during a round of play. You should also explain what actions are not permitted during the game, and how someone wins or loses.

____

____

____

____

____

____

____

____

____

Exchange your paper with your partner. Check one another's writing to make sure that your directions are complete and accurate. Then combine your best writing to complete a final draft of the directions for your game.

Student Exercise T-4

How to Make the Perfect Sandwich

It's lunchtime, and you're peering into a full refrigerator. Everything you need is right in front of you. It's time to make the world's best sandwich.

Write a clear, detailed, step-by-step set of instructions that will tell someone else how to make the perfect sandwich. Start by making some notes.

List all the ingredients you'll use:

____

____

____

What utensils will you need?

____

Now, list the steps, in order, that you'll take to assemble your creation:

____

____

____

____

How will you plate and serve your sandwich? What side dishes or garnish will you use?

____

____

Now, turn the notes above into a paragraph or paragraphs that tell someone how to create the perfect sandwich. After you've finished a first draft, exchange with a classmate. Make sure your instructions are clear, nothing has been left out and nothing extra has been added. Give each other feedback and suggestions.

Then write a final draft of your directions in paragraph form, using complete sentences.

50

Name _______________________________

How to . . .
Cook an egg, Change a diaper, Make coffee, Plant a tomato, Iron a shirt, Wash a car. . .

Each of us knows how to do many things well. After a while, these skills become so routine that we forget we once had to learn how the tasks were done. But we did have to learn. And now, it's your turn to pass that knowledge on to someone else.

Choose one of the tasks listed above. Or, choose another simple task—with your teacher's approval.

Write a clear, detailed, step-by-step set of instructions that will tell someone else how to accomplish the task you've chosen.

____

____

____

____

____

____

____

____

Once you've finished your directions, exchange with a classmate. Make sure nothing has been left out, and nothing extra has been added. Give each other feedback and suggestions.

Then write a final copy of your directions in paragraph form, using complete sentences.

Student Exercise T-6

Accessing Information on the Web

Suppose you wanted to find information about poison ivy on the World Wide Web. How would you go about it?

Assume that your classroom computer is turned off. List all the steps you would take, in the exact order you would do them, to locate information about this itchy subject.

____

____

____

____

____

____

____

____

____

Once you've finished your directions, exchange with a classmate. Your partner will then use your instructions to locate the information. Observe your classmate as he or she follows your directions. If your partner doesn't find the desired information, rewrite your directions to make them clearer and more precise.

Student Exercise T-7

Alien Instruction Manual

Can you use a can opener, a pencil sharpener or a door key? Of course! But what if you handed one of these objects to visitors from another planet—and they had never seen one before?

They'd need a set of instructions, naturally! That's what you're going to do—write directions that tell an alien how to use an ordinary, everyday object.

Start by brainstorming with your classmates. List some common household objects on the chalkboard. Make sure each one has at least one or two moving parts.

Then choose one object from the list you've brainstormed. Write a set of directions that tells how to use your object. Remember, you're writing for an alien who knows absolutely nothing about your object. He needs every detail you can give him.

HOW TO USE A ____

____

____

____

____

____

____

____

You didn't leave anything out, did you? Are all your instructions in the right order?

How good are your directions? Here's how to tell. Exchange papers with a friend. Take each other's paper home and try to follow the directions, exactly as they're written. Come back the next day and report what happened.

Name ___________________________

Map Directions
Starting Points and Destinations

Starting Point: Houston, TX Destination: Denver, CO	Starting Point: Atlanta, GA Destination: Buffalo, NY

Starting Point: Houston, TX
Destination: Denver, CO

Starting Point: Sacramento, CA
Destination: Spokane, WA

Starting Point: Bangor, ME
Destination: Cleveland, OH

Starting Point: Duluth, MN
Destination: Helena, MT

Starting Point: Richmond, VA
Destination: Jackson, MS

Starting Point: Pittsburgh, PA
Destination: Memphis, TN

Starting Point: Ottawa, Ontario
Destination: St. Paul, MN

Starting Point: Omaha, NE
Destination: Phoenix, AZ

Starting Point: San Diego, CA
Destination: Topeka, KS

Starting Point: Nashville, TN
Destination: Rapid City, SD

Starting Point: Portland, OR
Destination: Bismark, ND

Starting Point: Miami, FL
Destination: Little Rock, AR

Starting Point: St. Louis, MO
Destination: Charleston, SC

Starting Point: Atlanta, GA
Destination: Buffalo, NY

Starting Point: Boston, MA
Destination: Louisville, KY

Starting Point: Montreal, Quebec
Destination: Detroit, MI

Starting Point: Winnipeg, Manitoba
Destination: Great Falls, MT

Starting Point: Montgomery, AL
Destination: Baltimore, MD

Starting Point: Vancouver, B.C.
Destination: Salt Lake City, UT

Starting Point: Calgary, Alberta
Destination: Reno, NV

Starting Point: Albuquerque, NM
Destination: Chicago, IL

Starting Point: Charlotte, NC
Destination: Montpelier, VT

Starting Point: Charleston, WV
Destination: Milwaukee, WI

Starting Point: Laramie, WY
Destination: Tulsa, OK

Starting Point: Indianapolis, IN
Destination: Quebec, Quebec

Starting Point: Boise, ID
Destination: Santa Fe, NM

Expository Writing
Teacher Instructions

Expository Writing
(Student Exercises E-1 through E-3)

Each of these activities offers students a choice of two different topics to write about. Duplicate the exercises on the back
and front of a single sheet of paper, and allow students to
choose either of the assignments. Each exercise includes some
irrelevant information. Make sure students find and eliminate
irrelevant facts when they write their reports.

Use the "Technical/Expository Writing Evaluation Form" on
page 139 to give students feedback.

Independent Research Choices
(no student worksheet)

Have each student choose a topic of interest, research
and write a one-page report modeled on exercises E-1,
E-2 and E-3

Family Biography
(Student Exercise E-4)

Directions can be found on student exercise,
and should be self-explanatory.

Expository Writing: What's It Like?
(Student Exercise E-5)

Directions can be found on student exercise, and
should be self-explanatory.

Jewels of Wisdom
(Student Exercise E-6)

Directions can be found on student exercise, and should be self-explanatory.

Once students have completed their writings, you may want to share them with the people they interviewed, or post them on a "Wall of Fame" at your school. You can even invite your interviewees to a special, formal reception with your students. (Thanks to our colleague John Hunter for this activity.)

News Writing: The Inverted Pyramid
(Student Exercise E-7)

Materials: several copies of a newspaper; highlighting markers in several colors

In introducing this activity, have students examine stories in the newspaper to look for examples of the inverted pyramid style. Then have the students complete the activity on their worksheet.

As a follow-up, students may want to try reporting a real event for their school newspaper or class newsletter. If your class doesn't have a newsletter, this might be a good time to start one.

Expository Writing

Expository writing is writing that gives the reader information. Good expository writing should be clear and well organized. Don't include your own opinions. Just stick to the facts. Eliminate any information that is irrelevant to the topic.

Here are some notes about Mount Everest:

World's highest mountain.

Located in Asia.

Located on the border of Nepal and Tibet.

Mount Aconcagua in Argentina is the highest mountain in the Americas.

Mt. Everest is part of the Himalayas (mountain range).

Currently accepted measure of height: 29,028 feet.

Precise height is still in doubt.

Mount McKinley is also known by its Inuit name, Denali.

First successful ascent: Sir Edmund Hillary and Tenzing Norgay, 1953.

Has been climbed by hundreds of other climbers since 1953.

Write a report about Mount Everest that includes all the relevant information in the notes above. Make sure your writing is clear and well organized.

You do not have to organize your writing in the same order that the notes are presented, and you can combine two or more pieces of information in the same sentence.

Name _______________________

Expository Writing

Expository writing is writing that gives the reader information. Good expository writing should be clear and well organized. Don't include your own opinions. Just stick to the facts. Eliminate any information that is irrelevant to the topic.

Here are some notes about Benjamin Banneker:

Born 1731, Ellicott's Lower Mills, Maryland (now known as Ellicott City).

Son of a freed slave and a free African American woman.

Slavery ended in the United States in 1865, with the end of the Civil War.

Self-educated; had only a few years of elementary school.

Read books borrowed from a white neighbor.

In his early 20s built a wooden clock, without having seen a clock.

1771, began studying astronomy.

Correctly predicted a solar eclipse in 1789.

1791-1802 published the *Pennsylvania, Delaware, Maryland and Virginia Almanac*.

Benjamin Franklin was well known for his publication, *Poor Richard's Almanac*.

Appointed to the District of Columbia Commission by George Washington.

Drew the maps and plans for Washington, D.C., from memory, after designer Pierre L'Enfant withdrew from the project.

Died 1806, Baltimore County, Maryland.

Write a report about Benjamin Banneker that includes all the relevant information in the notes above. Make sure your writing is clear and well organized. You do not have to organize your writing in the same order that the notes are presented. However, writing about events in the sequence that they happened is often used as a way to organize a description of a person's life or accomplishments.

Student Exercise E-2

Expository Writing

Expository writing is writing that gives the reader information. Good expository writing should be clear and well organized. Don't include your own opinions. Just stick to the facts. Eliminate any information that is irrelevant to the topic, carbon.

Here are some notes about the element carbon:

Non-metallic chemical element.

Atomic number: 6.

Melting point: 3550°C.

Boiling point: 4827°C.

Sixth most common element in the universe.

Diamonds and graphite (the material of pencil leads) are both forms of carbon.

Bonds easily with many other elements.

More than six million different carbon compounds known, including sugars, starches, proteins, petroleum products and limestone.

Essential for life on Earth—contained in all plants and animals.

Life on Earth cannot exist without oxygen and nitrogen.

Plants take carbon—as carbon dioxide—from the air and combine it with water to form sugars and starches through the process of photosynthesis.

The carbon in activated charcoal can filter impurities from air or water.

The radioactive decay of carbon-14, an isotope of carbon, helps archaeologists date ancient objects.

Write a report about carbon that includes all the relevant information in the notes above. Make sure your writing is clear and well organized.   You do not have to organize your writing in the same order that the notes are presented.

59

Student Exercise E-2

Expository Writing

Expository writing is writing that gives the reader information. Good expository writing should be clear and well organized. Don't include your own opinions. Just stick to the facts. Eliminate any information that is irrelevant to the topic.

Here are some notes about quartz:

> Second most common mineral in the Earth's crust.
> Comes in many forms.
> The Earth's core is thought to be made of molten iron and other metals.
> Composed of silicon dioxide.
> Greek name for clear quartz: *krystallos*—source of the English word *crystal*.
> Diamond crystals are the hardest substance known.
> Most sand is made up of quartz.
> Quartz is found in granite, flint, sandstone and quartzite.
> Gemstone forms include amethyst, rose quartz, agate and citrine.
> Used in abrasives, grindstones and polishing powders.
> Quartz sand is the main ingredient in glass.
> Vibrating quartz crystals are used in electronics such as clocks, radios and televisions.
> Quartz crystals are grown in laboratories for scientific and technical uses.

Write a report about quartz that includes all the relevant information in the notes above. Make sure your writing is clear and well organized.   You do not have to organize your writing in the same order that the notes are presented.

Expository Writing

Expository writing is writing that gives the reader information. Good expository writing should be clear and well organized. Don't include your own opinions. Just stick to the facts. Eliminate any information that is irrelevant to the topic.

Here are some notes about the violin:

> Member of the string family, that also includes viola, cello and double bass.
>
> First built in early 16th century.
>
> Since that time string instruments have become the most important part of symphony orchestras and smaller ensembles.
>
> A concerto is a piece of music for orchestra and a featured solo instrument.
>
> Pianos and harps are usually considered members of the percussion family.
>
> Violin has four strings attached to pegs.
>
> Strings are tuned by turning the pegs.
>
> Sound produced by bowing or plucking strings.
>
> Sound resonates in the hollow body of the instrument.
>
> F-holes cut in top of violin allow sound waves to escape.
>
> Back, neck and ribs (sides) of violin made of maple, top made of spruce.
>
> Greatest violins were built in Italian town of Cremona, by Antonio Stradivari and several others.
>
> Modern violinmakers still follow the designs created by the great Italian builders.

Write a report about the violin that includes all the relevant information in the notes above. Make sure your writing is clear and well organized.   You do not have to organize your writing in the same order that the notes are presented.

Student Exercise E-3

Expository Writing

Expository writing is writing that gives the reader information. Good expository writing should be clear and well organized. Don't include your own opinions. Just stick to the facts. Eliminate any information that is irrelevant to the topic.

Here are some notes about Galileo Galilei:

Born Pisa, Italy, 1564.

Pisa is famous for its leaning tower.

Died in Florence, Italy, 1642.

Often known just by first name.

Considered the founder of experimental science.

1583—Discovered law of pendulum motion. Made first accurate clocks possible.

Discovered the law of acceleration for falling objects.

1609—Built a telescope and discovered four moons orbiting Jupiter—first direct evidence of other heavenly bodies orbiting one another.

Discovered craters and mountains on the moon.

Discovered that the Milky Way is made of many individual stars.

Punished by the Catholic Church for supporting the theory that the Earth revolves around the sun. Spent last eight years of life under house arrest for this belief.

Isaac Newton was known for formulating the law of universal gravitation.

Write a report about Galileo that includes all the relevant information in the notes above. Make sure your writing is clear and well organized.   You do not have to organize your writing in the same order that the notes are presented.

62

Name ___________________________

Family Biography

Tell us about your parent or guardian. First, you'll need to gather some biographical information. Interview your parent or guardian, using the guide below.

Birth date: _______________________   Birthplace: _______________________

Parents: ____

Details about your parents' parents: _______________________________________

____

____

Occupation: ____

Details about work: ____

____

____

Hobbies, skills and interests: ____

____

____

What things/ideas does your parent value most? _______________________________

____

Personal goals: ____

____

Other information (your choice of questions): _________________________________

____

____

Once you've gathered your information, write a report that tells about your parent or guardian. Revise and write a final draft to share.

Student Exercise E-5

Expository Writing: What's It Like?

Think of some unusual things you've done—something that other people in your class might not have experienced. Have you climbed on a ropes course, eaten at a Vietnamese restaurant or performed in a play or recital? Perhaps you've ridden a horse or rescued someone. Try to think of several different unusual experiences you've had.

List them. ____

____

Now, choose one, and tell what the experience was like. Explain how you came to be in the situation.

____

____

Describe what happened, step by step. ___________________________________

____

____

Tell us about the sensations you had. What did it feel like? Describe the smells, sights and sounds.

____

____

What did you think about during the experience? Afterwards?_________________

____

____

How did the experience affect your emotions? What did it feel like?_____________

____

Are you glad you had this experience? Did you learn anything? Would you do it again?_____________

____

Now, take all the ideas you've collected above, and turn them into an essay that will share your experience with others.

Student Exercise E-6

Jewels of Wisdom
Honoring the Senior Members of Our Community

Your assignment is to write about a senior member of your community, outside your immediate family. First identify someone to write about. Remember, everyone is interesting if you look closely enough.

Your next step will be to gather information and take notes. You will have to interview your subject, observe and ask questions. You may want to use a tape recorder while you speak with your subject. Find out:

- ❑ Basic biographical information: full name; age; birth date and birthplace; current home; family members; education; and employment history.

- ❑ Special or unusual accomplishments.

- ❑ Hobbies, interests and community involvement.

- ❑ Philosophy and values. What are the most important rules your subject has followed in his or her life?

- ❑ Interesting events from your subject's life.

- ❑ What that person considers the most important events during his or her lifetime.

Listen carefully, and follow up with more questions to gather more details.

After your interview, take notes that describe:

- ❑ Physical appearance, speech and behavior of your subject.

- ❑ Typical gestures and phrases that your subject uses.

Find at least one other person who knows your subject. Interview that person and gather more information and stories for your biography.

Now, write a first draft of your biography. Try starting with an interesting quotation from, or about your subject. Or introduce your subject by telling a story about something he or she has done. You do not have to use all the data you've gathered. Choose the information that will keep your readers interested.

Finally, revise your biography and write your final draft.

Student Exercise E-7

News Writing: The Inverted Pyramid

When reporters write a story, they don't know how much space will be allotted for it in the newspaper. So they must place the most important information in the first part of their article. They leave less important, but interesting facts for the end. This allows the last part of the article to be cut, if necessary. The story can fit in a smaller space in the newspaper without losing any essential information.

This style of writing is often compared to an inverted pyramid. The base of the pyramid is on top—representing the most important facts. As the pyramid tapers to a point, the facts in the story become less important. This kind of writing also helps busy readers who may not have time to read the entire article. Reading just the first few paragraphs gives them the most important facts. Unlike other writing styles, the author doesn't wait until the end to summarize, make a point or solve a mystery.

Try writing a story using the inverted pyramid form. Use one of the sets of facts below. Of course, reporters are allowed to use only facts, but you can use your imagination to fill in extra details. State the most important facts first, but write so the reader will want to finish the whole article. When you are finished, exchange stories with a partner. Ask your partner to highlight the important facts with a light colored marker. Ask him or her to highlight interesting, but nonessential information with a different colored marker.

Set 1
Who: singer, Jesse Bright and 10-year-old fan, Eddie Alt
When: Saturday, June 15, after Bright's concert
Where: backstage at the Cleveland Theater
What: Bright invited the fan to meet and have dinner with the band.
Why: Eddie Alt had written a fan letter to Bright.

Set 2
Who: elephant trainer, Calvin Hodges; elephant Katie
When: Sunday, February 25, immediately after closing performance of the circus
Where: outside the Coliseum where animals were being loaded into trucks
What: Katie sat on, and crushed a small car parked on the street where the animals were walking to the trucks.
Why: trainer Hodges is puzzled by Katie's behavior, says she must "have been tired after three performances today."

Set 3
Who: NFL player, Emmit Brown
When: Friday, February 6, during 7th period
Where: River's Edge Middle School
What: Brown made a surprise visit to Mr. Cable's class.
Why: Mr. Cable had told class that Brown was a former student. The class wrote to Brown saying how proud Cable was of Brown's accomplishments and asking for an autographed picture for the classroom. Brown responded with the surprise visit.

Introduce this unit of the writing curriculum by distributing copies of the student guide, "Personal Essays," on page 68. Discuss how writing effective personal essays can help students get into the school of their choice, or get a job they want. Remind them that colleges, magnet high school programs, many special summer programs and employment applications often require essays of this kind.

Students must sometimes complete personal essays within a limited time, in a test-like setting. If you expect your students will have to write under time constraints, have them follow similar limits as they complete these assignments. Otherwise, you can ease the time restrictions for at least some of their writing.

Review how to use webs or mind-maps, outlines and other graphic organizers as planning tools for students' writing.

When making each writing assignment, duplicate the assignment sheets and cut them apart, or put the two to three alternative prompts on the board. Before students begin writing, hand out copies of the "Personal Essay Evaluation Form" on page 137, so they will know in advance how their work will be evaluated.

When you find examples of well-written student work, have the writer share that part of his or her essay with the class. This will reinforce the kinds of writing behaviors you are trying to promote. When a weak writer is praised for even one beautiful sentence, he or she will try to write more.

For the First Assignment

Structure students' time for them. Give them five minutes to make a web or outline before they begin writing. Allow at least 20-30 minutes to create a first draft.

On the following day, have them write a second draft, and exchange with a partner. Partners should give feedback using the "Personal Essay Evaluation Form" on page 137.

Then have students write a final draft and turn it in for teacher evaluation. Teachers should evaluate using the same form.

Subsequent Assignments

Encourage students to structure their own time. Remind them to brainstorm, web or outline first. Give them one class period to write a first draft, and a second period to produce a final draft.

Then have students exchange papers with a partner for evaluation. Remind students that you reserve the right to overrule their evaluations if you think they are too harsh or too lenient.

Have students staple their evaluations to their final drafts. For teacher evaluation, review student evaluations and modify as necessary.

Student Guide

Personal Essays

The personal essay assignments will help you prepare to answer questions on applications for selective high schools, special summer programs or even for a job.

These writing tasks usually start with a "prompt," a simple question for you to answer. These prompts are ordinarily very general. For example, a prompt may ask, "What historical figure do you admire most and why?" or "What do you expect to be doing 10 years from now?" These are broad questions that allow you to express your own opinions, and display your own values and personality.

Prompts like these don't give much information. So your first step should be to think. Don't start writing immediately. Do some brainstorming, and organize your thoughts. Make an outline or a web, or simply jot down a list of ideas that come to mind. Give yourself at least five minutes to think before you write the first sentence.

The people who will evaluate your writing will be looking for good organization. Start your essay with a strong topic sentence. One way to do this is by rearranging and using the words in the original prompt. Look at the examples above. A good topic sentence for the first one might be "The historical figure I admire most is ________." or "Of all the people I've read about in history, I think ________ is the person I admire most." For the second prompt, you could start by writing "Ten years from now, I plan to be ________." or "In 10 years, I would like to be ________."

Support your topic sentence with at least two or three reasons. Be specific and include several details that support each reason. Make sure to connect the details to the main idea logically. That's something else the evaluators will be looking for.

In the first example, suppose you chose Thomas Jefferson. Here are some good supporting sentences: "I admire Jefferson for his curiosity and creativity. He spent many years experimenting with different kinds of crops, and invented labor-saving devices for his home, Monticello." Those specific details support the essay's main idea.

Finally, close your essay with a sentence that lets the reader know you're finished. Bring the reader back to the original idea. For example, you might say, "If I could meet any one historical figure, I would certainly choose our third President."

Even when your time is limited, it's a good idea to write a rough draft first. Then make revisions before you complete the final product. If your time is very limited, it might be wise to write with a pencil or erasable pen so you can make corrections without crossing out. Remember, an essay shows people what kind of worker you are. A well-organized, careful, thorough essay tells them you are a well-organized, careful, thorough worker.

Finally, don't forget the importance of legible penmanship. You probably won't be using a word processor. Before your writing can be evaluated, it must be read. Sloppy work also leaves the impression that you are careless or don't take pride in your work—which is certainly not an idea you want to leave with the readers who are evaluating you.

Personal Essay Writing Prompts

Set 1: Choose one of the following topics to write about:

Create a first draft.

Revise and write a second draft.

Then exchange with a partner. Partners should give feedback using the "Personal Essay Evaluation Form."

Write a final draft to turn in for your teacher's evaluation.

—Describe what you hope your life will be like one year, 10 years and 25 years from now.

—Describe the one person who has had the most influence on your life. Explain what that person has meant to you.

—If you had to spend a month alone, what three items would you choose to take with you? Explain.

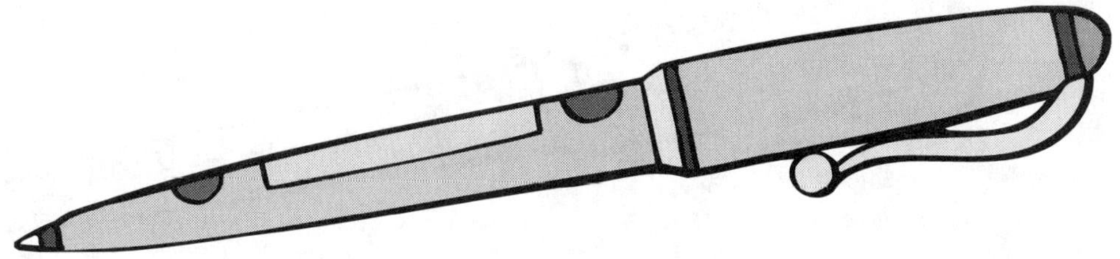

Student Exercise P-2

Personal Essay Writing Prompts

Set 2: Choose one of the following topics to write about:

Create a first draft.

Revise and write a second draft.

Then exchange with a partner. Partners should give feedback using the "Personal Essay Evaluation Form."

Write a final draft to turn in for your teacher's evaluation.

—What historical figure do you admire most, and why?

—If you could bring to life and meet any character from literature, who would you choose, and why?

—What do you think is the most important invention of the past 100 years?

Personal Essay Writing Prompts

Set 3: Choose one of the following topics to write about:

Create a first draft.

Revise and write a second draft.

Then exchange with a partner. Partners should give feedback using the "Personal Essay Evaluation Form."

Finally, write a final draft to turn in for your teacher's evaluation.

—What are your career goals?

—What qualities do you think are most important in a good student (or a good employee)?

—Describe your ideal job.

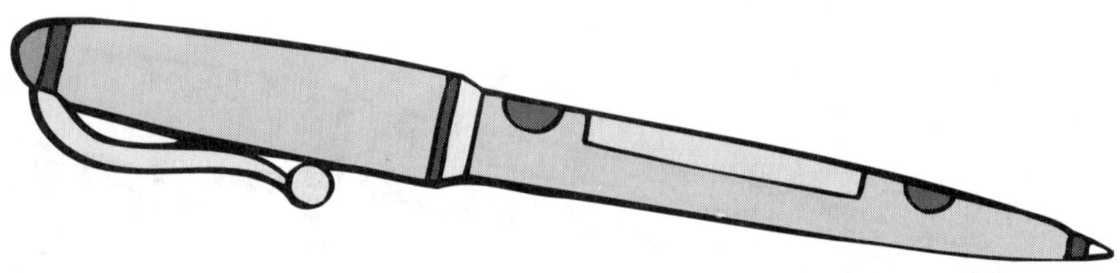

Student Exercise P-4

Personal Essay Writing Prompts

Set 4: Choose one of the following topics to write about:

Create a first draft.

Revise and write a second draft.

Then exchange with a partner. Partners should give feedback using the "Personal Essay Evaluation Form."

Write a final draft to turn in for your teacher's evaluation.

—What qualities do you have that make you a valuable member of your school community?

—What effect would you like your life to have on the world, and how do you plan to achieve that goal?

—If you could choose one color (or building, or piece of music) to describe your personality, what would it be?

Personal Essay Writing Prompts

Set 5: Choose one of the following topics to write about:

Create a first draft.

Revise and write a second draft.

Then exchange with a partner. Partners should give feedback using the "Personal Essay Evaluation Form."

Write a final draft to turn in for your teacher's evaluation.

—Describe yourself through the eyes of someone else who knows you well—a teacher, a parent or a good friend, for example.

—Explain how you faced and overcame an obstacle in your life.

—Describe an incident that changed the way you look at life.

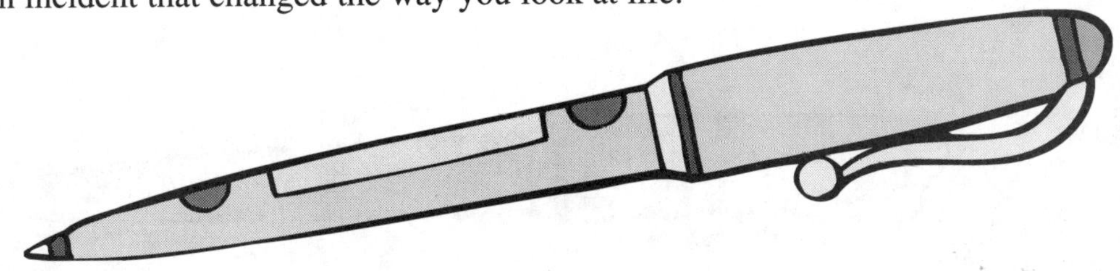

Student Exercise P-6

Personal Essay Writing Prompts

Set 6: Choose one of the following topics to write about:

Create a first draft.

Revise and write a second draft.

Then exchange with a partner. Partners should give feedback using the "Personal Essay Evaluation Form."

Write a final draft to turn in for your teacher's evaluation.

—What is your most treasured possession and why is it so important to you?

—If you could spend a month anywhere in the world, where would you choose to go, and why?

—Imagine yourself 50 years from now. Write a biography that describes how you have spent your life, and what you have accomplished.

Personal Essay Writing Prompts

Set 7: Choose one of the following topics to write about:

Create a first draft.

Revise and write a second draft.

Then exchange with a partner. Partners should give feedback using the "Personal Essay Evaluation Form."

Write a final draft to turn in for your teacher's evaluation.

—What was the most difficult challenge you've ever faced, and how did you respond to it?

—What are your most important responsibilities as a citizen? How have you prepared yourself in order to fulfill those responsibilities?

—If you could change the world in one way, what would you do and why?

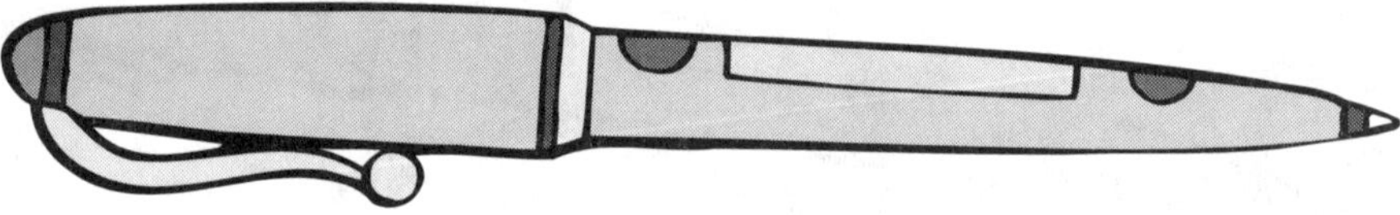

Student Exercise P-8

Personal Essay Writing Prompts

Set 8: Choose one of the following topics to write about:

Create a first draft.

Revise and write a second draft.

Then exchange with a partner. Partners should give feedback using the "Personal Essay Evaluation Form."

Write a final draft to turn in for your teacher's evaluation.

—What are the most essential principles people should follow as they live their lives? Explain why you think these rules are important.

—If you could change one thing about your life, what would you do, and why?

—Describe the accomplishment in your life that you are most proud of.

Essay writing requires students to think critically and logically. It should also help prepare students to respond more successfully to essay questions on tests. As they advance through their academic careers, students will be evaluated more and more frequently on their ability to write well-organized, thoughtful essays.

How to Make an Essay Sandwich

The "Essay Sandwich" is a visual reminder to help students organize their essay. They can think of their essay as a sandwich.

The top slice is the main idea, the statement of their thesis or opinion.

Inside is the "meat" of their essay—their reasons for their opinion.

Each reason should be backed up with the "condiments" of supporting details, facts that help prove their case.

Finally, the bottom slice of bread represents the closing, that restates or summarizes the writer's main idea or opinion.

Enlarge this graphic. Post it in your room and explain it to the students. Then refer students to it as you introduce a new essay topic, or when a student has problems organizing his or her writing.

This is a visual aid that really helps students organize their writing. We'd like to thank the educator who first devised this idea, whoever that may be. We've been unable to discover the identity of the original creator.

Identifying Factual and Hypothetical Examples
(Student Exercise O-1)

Have students read the "Essays of Opinion" student worksheet on page 78. Make sure they understand the concept of a hypothetical example, and that examples from real-world events always carry more weight. Exercise O-1 will give them additional practice recognizing the difference between hypothetical and factual examples. (1, 2, 5 and 8 are hypothetical.)

Essays of Opinion
(Student Exercise O-2)

This activity can be assigned several times using different topics. The first time you present this assignment, you may want to introduce it as a whole-class activity, perhaps using a transparency and overhead projector.

Base the assignments in this section on short essays you find in the newspaper or news magazines. Copies of newspaper editorials, op-ed (opposite the editorial page) essays and letters to the editor are great places to find ideas to stimulate student writing.

Search for topics that will be of particular interest to students—popular culture, school violence or sports issues for example. You can also ask students to be on the lookout for interesting articles to write about.

Whenever you make this assignment, give students a choice of at least two different topics. This lesson should be used several times—although not necessarily consecutively—to help students develop the skill of expressing their opinions clearly and effectively. Give the students different topic choices each time.

You Said It!
(Student Exercise O-3)

Writers, philosophers and speakers have provided us with a wealth of interesting and controversial quotations. These sayings can serve as stimuli for student writings.

This is an activity that can be used on any number of occasions. Whether it's history, science, literature or mathematics, relevant quotations can stimulate students to think and write. You can always find quotations that take a variety of viewpoints on any issue. That makes for controversy, and heightens interest.

Most books of quotations are indexed by subject and author. The reference section of your local library or school media center should have several volumes, each containing thousands of quotations on almost every subject imaginable. There are also internet sites which catalog quotations by the thousands.

To get your students writing, collect several quotations on a particular topic. Display them on the board or bulletin board ahead of time. Discuss the meaning of each quotation with the class before you ask them to start writing.

To get you started, we've provided a few select quotations on (pages 83-85) on several subjects from among thousands—freedom, justice and self-respect. But don't stop there. "You Said It!" can be used as an introductory activity for almost any instructional unit.

Students as Reviewers
(Student Exercises O-5 through O-8)

Making judgements and committing them to paper are important critical thinking and writing skills. It's easiest when students write about things they know—things they already have begun to form opinions about. New toys or games, books, foods or TV shows make ideal topics for students to evaluate.

Most students already have a sense of what a professional reviewer does. They have seen movie reviewers on television or read reviews in magazines and newspapers. Before you ask students to write their own reviews, spend some class time looking at videotaped movie reviews; and restaurant, movie, theatre and book reviews from newspapers and magazines.

Reviewing a TV show is probably most appropriate for fall, after the new television season has gotten underway. Kids are tuning in the new programs anyway and deciding whether or not they like them. Take advantage of that interest by turning it into a writing lesson.

The toy and game reviews might work best in January, after the holidays, when students have had a chance to try out their new playthings. Most students will be glad to bring in one of their newest toys or games from home.

The restaurant review of your school cafeteria food could be done almost anytime during the year. What students wouldn't relish the chance to tell the truth about the food they're served each day?

For best results, students need time to use the games and toys, watch the programs or sample the lunches before they write. Be generous! Students can't judge a TV show fairly on the basis of one episode. A full hour or more of play with the toys and games will pay off in higher-quality writing. Give students the guide sheets ahead of time, so they will know what to look for as they watch or play.

Encourage students to choose a game or toy that they have never used before. Similarly, they should choose a TV show that is new to them. And encourage students to try new and unfamiliar dishes when they review the cafeteria, too. Of course, students must also draw on past experiences with other shows, games and meals in order to make comparisons in their writing.

Remind students that filling out the exercise sheets is just the first step in the process. The end product should be revised into a polished, well-organized essay that could be published in the school newspaper.

Writing Prompts for Essays of Opinion

Should we change to a year-round school calendar (nine weeks on/three weeks off)?

Block scheduling: is it a good plan?

Should college athletes be paid? Should they be required to meet minimum criteria for entrance into colleges and universities?

Every student should be supplied with a laptop computer. Agree or disagree?

At what age should young people be allowed to vote (or drive, or drink alcohol)?

Should public school students be required to wear uniforms?

Should students be required to participate in school fund-raisers?

Should all students be required to take physical education each year?

Should organized prayer be a part of every public school day?

Should adolescents who commit violent crimes be tried as adults?

Does yearly standardized testing make the public schools better?

Should we end court-ordered desegregation and cross-town busing in American schools?

Would American students benefit if they could attend single-sex middle schools?

If I were Superintendent of Schools and could make three (and only three) changes to immediately improve the schools, they would be . . .

If I were the Secretary of Education of the United States and I could change every American public school, the most important thing I would change would be . . .

American schools are facing a shortage of teachers. Write an essay telling someone why they should (or should not) become a teacher in an American public school.

Many American schools remain empty from 2:30 p.m. until 8 a.m. What would you do to utilize the buildings in order to make our cities better, safer, smarter places?

How could we improve the variety and quality of meals served to school children?

If you could honor someone with a monument, who would you select and why?

Should the U.S. national anthem be changed to "America the Beautiful"?

Essay Sandwich

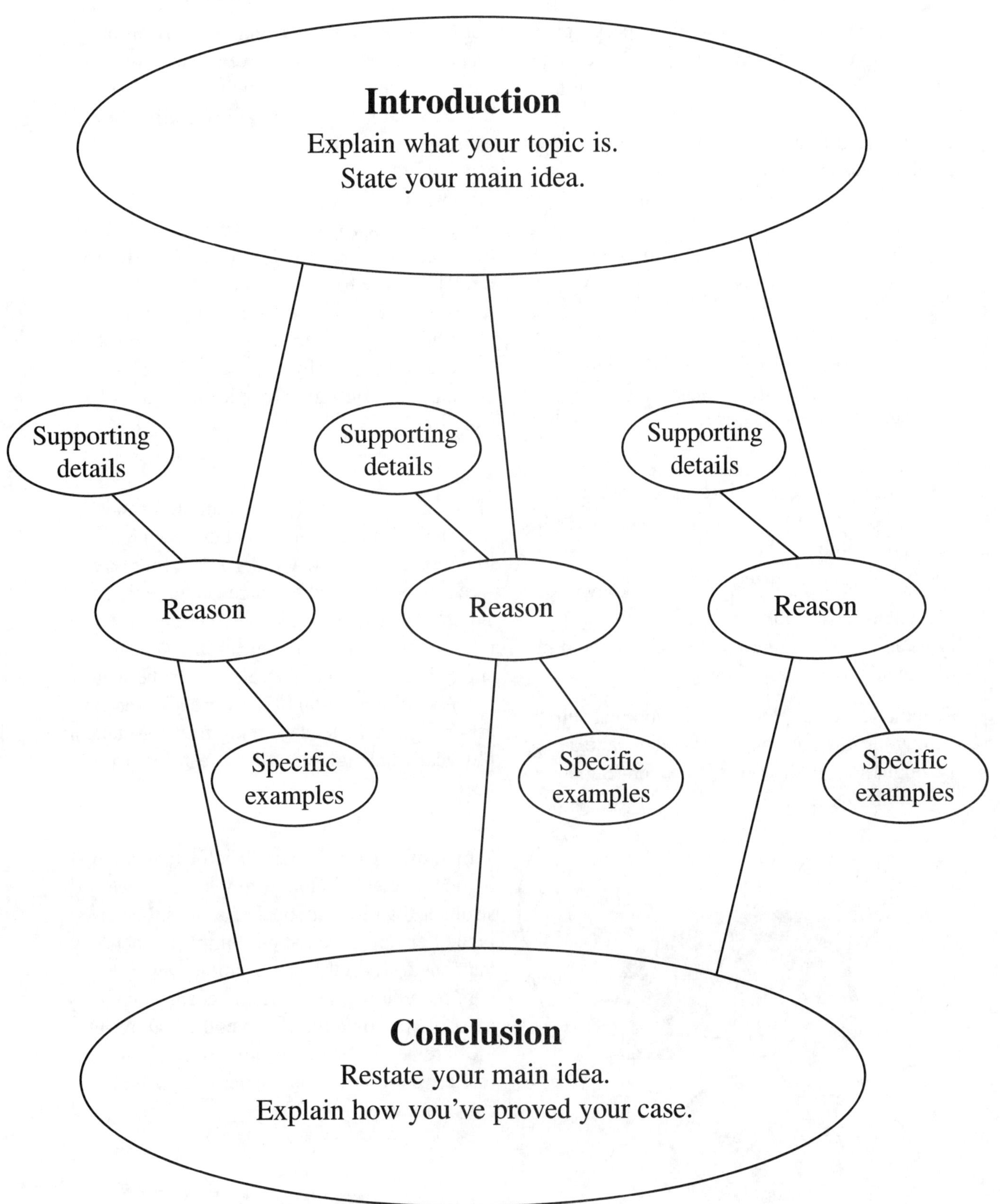

Essays of Opinion

Essays of opinion—as you might expect—give you an opportunity to say what you think about a topic. When you write an essay of opinion, you should:

1. State your opinion clearly.
2. Give reasons for your opinion.
3. Support your reasons with details and examples.
4. Summarize your opinion, in different words, at the conclusion of your essay.

Your essay will be stronger if you also:

5. Anticipate opposing argument(s), and answer them by giving reasons why your viewpoint is stronger.

There are two different kinds of examples you can use to support your opinions: factual examples and hypothetical examples.

Factual examples are things that are known to be true. You can look them up in a history book, an almanac, a newspaper or find them in your own personal experience.

Hypothetical examples are ones you make up using your imagination. A hypothetical example might start with "What if . . ." or "Suppose . . ." or "Imagine . . ."

For example, you're writing an essay arguing that students should not have to take physical education class if they participate in other organized athletics. Here are two different examples you might use:

Hypothetical

"Suppose a boy was on the soccer, football and track teams at his neighborhood recreation center. He'd have to go to practice three or four times a week. He'd spend at least seven or eight hours exercising each week. Why should he need to be in a physical education class at school, too? He's already getting plenty of exercise."

Factual

"Lauren Harris, a girl at my church, is an excellent gymnast. She practices with her gymnastics coach two hours a day, four days a week. Both she and her parents agree that she's healthy and strong. She is already getting plenty of physical education. At school, she'd like to take another elective. She would get a better education if she were allowed take art or French, instead of being forced to take a physical education class she doesn't really need.

Which example is better? The factual example is much better. Factual examples are always stronger than hypothetical examples, because factual examples tell about things that actually happened. Hypothetical examples *might* happen, but you can't be certain because they only exist in your own mind. Hypothetical examples are better than no examples at all, but factual examples are much better than hypothetical examples.

Name _______________________________________

Identifying Factual and Hypothetical Examples

Here are some examples taken from essays of opinion. For each one, decide whether it is a hypothetical example or a factual example. Write an H or an F beside each one to indicate your choice.

_________ 1. Suppose someone was found guilty of murder and sentenced to death because a witness was afraid to come forward and testify that someone else had committed the crime. If that person were to be executed, the government would be executing an innocent man.

_________ 2. What if you didn't have enough money to buy medicine for your sick child? Would you still consider stealing a crime?

_________ 3. You don't always have to play basketball in college in order to have a successful career in the NBA. For example, both Kobe Bryant and Kevin Garnett became professional players right after high school. Neither of them played college ball, and both of them were stars within just a couple of years.

_________ 4. Sometimes a publishing company can make lots of money from printing material that is no longer copyrighted. Companies have made millions of dollars publishing copies of the Bible; other companies have made their fortune publishing calendars. Both the Bible and the calendar are "in the public domain." That means no one owns the copyright to them.

_________ 5. Can physical ability be a reasonable requirement for some occupations? Of course. Suppose someone with 20/600 eyesight decided to become a pilot. Would you want to travel with that person flying the airplane?

_________ 6. You don't have to have a college education to get a good job, but it helps. Sure, Bill Gates never finished college and he's a billionaire. But my Uncle Curtis didn't finish college either. He's 40 years old, and he's never had a job that paid more than 10 dollars an hour. He told me that if he could do it all over again, he'd stay in school until he finished.

_________ 7. Some plants die after they have produced their fruit and seeds. For example, pineapple plants produce their fruit on a tall stalk. Once the fruit has ripened or been picked, the plant dies. Similarly, a banana plant dies after it has flowered and produced a crop of ripe bananas. Once these plants have produced a crop, their task in life is done.

_________ 8. We know that there's life on Earth. But there are probably millions of other planets elsewhere in the universe. Surely some of these other worlds have the right chemical elements and the right temperatures to support life. And if that's true, couldn't some kind of life have evolved on at least some of them? Perhaps some of that life has evolved intelligence greater than our own.

Name _______________________

Essays of Opinion

I. Carefully read the current events essay you have chosen.

II. What is the author's main point?

____

____

____

III. What are the main facts or reasons the author uses to support his or her point?

____

____

____

III. Do you ___ agree or ___disagree? Why? Explain your reasons.

____

____

____

____

____

Student Exercise O-2 (continued)

IV. If you agree, choose at least two ideas or statements that you think are particularly strong. Think of your own reasons and examples to support those ideas.

If you disagree, select two or three ideas or statements that you disagree with most strongly. Think of your own reasons and examples to support your opposing viewpoint.

____

____

____

____

____

____

____

Finally, summarize your own viewpoint on the issue.

____

____

____

____

____

Now, use these ideas to write your own essay on the topic.

Name ______________________

You Said It!

Through history, men and women have said many wise, clever or thought-provoking things about many different subjects. You may agree with some of these quotations completely. Others you may disagree with.

You have been given a group of quotations about a particular subject. Choose the one that you agree with (or disagree with) most strongly.

Which quotation did you choose?

____

____

In your own words, explain what the author means in this quotation.

____

____

Explain why you think this idea is true (or false).

____

____

Think of some examples from real life which illustrate the idea in your quotation.

____

____

What would someone who disagreed say about this quotation?

____

____

How would you respond to that argument?

____

____

What is the importance or value of the idea in this quotation?

____

____

Look back at what you've written. Rearrange your ideas to create an interesting, well-organized essay. Then write a final copy of your essay.

You Said It! Freedom

"Better to die on one's feet than live on one's knees."
—Dolores Ibarruri

"Those who expect to reap the blessings of freedom must . . . undergo the fatigue of supporting it."
—Thomas Paine

"I know but one freedom, and that is the freedom of the mind."
—Antoine de Saint-Exupery

"Freedom cannot be granted [given]. It must be taken."
—Max Stirner

"We are not free . . . . A book of rules is placed in our cradle, and we never get rid of it until we reach our graves."
—E.W. Howe

"Perfect freedom is reserved for the man who lives by his own work and in that work does what he wants to do."
—R.G. Collingwood

"Freedom's just another word for nothin' left to lose."
—Kris Kristofferson

"A man is either free or he is not. There cannot be any apprentice-ship for freedom."
—Imamu Amiri Baraka (LeRoi Jones)

"My definition of a free society is a society where it is safe to be unpopular."
—Adlai Stevenson

"It is often better to be in chains than to be free."
—Franz Kafka

You Said It! Justice

"It is better to suffer injustice than to do it."
—Ralph Waldo Emerson

"What's sauce for the goose is sauce for the gander."
—Anonymous

"One hour doing justice is worth a hundred in prayer."
—Islamic proverb

"Only the just man enjoys peace of mind."
—Epicurus

"Justice delayed is justice denied."
—Legal axiom

"Justice must be observed, even to the lowliest."
—Cicero

"Justice is truth in action."
—Benjamin Disraeli

"Injustice anywhere is a threat to justice everywhere."
—Dr. M. L. King Jr.

"There is no such thing as justice—in or out of court."
—Clarence Darrow

Injustice is relatively easy to bear; what stings is justice."
—H. L. Mencken

"One man's justice is another's injustice."
—Ralph Waldo Emerson

You Said It! Self-Respect

"Self-confidence is the first requisite to great undertakings"
—Samuel Johnson

"If you wish to know yourself, observe how others act. If you wish
to understand others, look into your own heart"
—Schiller

"He that respects himself is safe from others.
He wears a coat of mail that none can pierce."
—Longfellow

"We are what people say we are. We know ourselves chiefly by
hearsay."
—Eric Hoffer

"Everyone should measure himself by his own standard and measure-
ment."
—Horace

"Be always displeased with what thou art if thou desirest to become
what thou art not."
—Francis Quarles

"Self-love is the greatest of all flatterers."
—La Rochefoucauld

"We confide in our strength, without boasting of it; we respect that of
others, without fearing it."
—Thomas Jefferson

"You gain strength, courage and confidence by every experience in
which you really stop to look fear in the face."
—Anna Eleanor Roosevelt

Name ________________________

Problem/Solution Essay

One way to organize an essay of opinion is to describe and discuss a problem, and then present one or more ways to solve it.

Choose a problem in your school, community or country that you would like to write about.

____

____

Describe the problem in more detail. What harm does it do? Whom does it affect?

____

____

____

List as many causes of that problem as you can.

____

____

____

Now, think of several possible ways to solve or improve the problem.

____

____

____

Which solutions do you think will work best? Explain why.

____

____

____

Look back at what you've written. Rearrange your ideas so that they will make an interesting, well-organized essay. Then write a final copy of your essay.

Student Exercise O-5

Reviews: Our School Cafeteria
A User's Guide

Restaurant critics advise people about places where they might go out to eat. They tell readers what kind of food and service to expect. A critic should always be fair. He or she must include both the good and the bad. That way, readers learn to trust the critic's opinions.

Suppose you were reviewing the eating place you know best—the school cafeteria. What would you say? Here's your chance! Of course, everyone likes to joke about cafeteria food—but be fair!

List some of the best foods that the cafeteria serves. ____

____

____

Describe in detail one dish that you recommend especially. _____________________________________

____

____

List some foods that the cafeteria doesn't prepare very well. __________________________________

____

____

Describe in detail one dish that is particularly poor. ____

____

____

Describe the service in your cafeteria. ____

____

Is the cafeteria a pleasant place to eat? Describe its atmosphere. ____________________________

____

____

What improvements should be made to make it a better place to eat?______________________________

____

____

Revise and rewrite your review in the form of an essay.

Toy or Game Review

Movie reviewers tell you a little bit about a movie. Then they analyze what they like and don't like about it. Finally, they give you an evaluation—is it worth spending your time and money to see it? Since tastes vary, they also consider who might enjoy it. Books, records, TV shows and new products also get reviewed.

You're going to write a review about a new game or toy. Before you write, read the rules or directions for the toy carefully. Then play with it until you feel familiar with it.

Name of toy: ____   Price: ____________

Company that produces it: ____

Person who invented or designed it (if available): ___________________________________

Purpose of the toy or game (What is it supposed to do for people who use it?): ____________

____

Describe how it works. ____

____

____

How hard is it to learn to use? ____

____

What do you like about it? What are its best features? _______________________________

____

____

How sturdy is it? Will it stand up to frequent use? _________________________________

____

Does it require extra expenses for batteries, additional pieces, etc.? ____________________

What don't you like, or how might you change it to make it better? _____________________

____

Your recommendations: Who would like this toy or game? Is it worth the money? Is it fun? Does it keep your interest?

Is there anything else you want to say about the toy or game? Revise and rewrite your review in final form.

Movie or TV Review

Reviewers tell you more than whether or not they like a movie or TV show. They give you enough information about the plot and characters so you can decide whether or not you want to see it. Your assignment is to review a movie or television show. Choose a movie or show you know well and have seen recently. If it's available on video or DVD, watch it again before you complete this project.

Name of movie or show: _______________________________   Director: _______________________________

Featured actors: _______________________________

Screenwriter: _______________________________

Describe the setting of the movie or show. Where and when does it take place? _______________________________

____

Describe the main characters. Who are they, what are their personalities like and which actors play them?

____

____

In a paragraph, describe the plot. Tell what the story is about without giving away the ending. _______________

____

____

____

Describe anything else of importance about it (scenery, action, music, etc.). _______________________________

____

____

What do you like most about the movie or show? _______________________________

What do you not like about it? How could it have been improved? _______________________________

____

Your recommendation: Will other people enjoy this movie or show? Will it appeal to a particular group?

____

Is there anything else you want to say about it? Revise and rewrite your review in final form.

Student Exercise O-8

Textbook Review

How good are your textbooks? Are they well organized? Interesting to read? Useful? Let's analyze one and find out. Choose any one of your textbooks to review. Remember, reviewers are critical but fair.

Name of book: ____   Subject: _________________________________

Author(s): ____   Publisher: _______________________________

Topics covered in book: ____

What reference resources does it include (glossary, index, appendix, etc.)? ____________________________

____

How well is it written? Is it interesting to read? Are the reading level and vocabulary appropriate for your age

group? ____

____

Does it explain things clearly? Is it easy to understand?____

Does it ask questions, and are the questions helpful? ____

What are the illustrations like? Are they clear and informative? Do they help readers understand the ideas in

the book? ____

What do you think of the page layout? Is it attractive, cluttered, too plain, etc.? ___________________________

____

Does the text and the illustrations represent the racial and ethnic diversity of the country, and diversity of

thought or opinion? ____

What do you like about it? What are its best features? ____

What don't you like, or how might you change it to make it better? _______________________________________

____

Your recommendations: Should the school system continue to use this book, or should it be replaced with a

better one? ____

Is there anything else you want to say about the book? Revise and rewrite your review in final form.

Descriptive Writing

Teacher Instructions

Know Your Apple
(no student worksheet)

Materials
large bowl
apple (orange, walnut or banana, etc.) for
    each student
large roll of paper

Each student takes an apple. Tell them they'll be able to eat the fruit, but not yet.

Have students spend about five minutes carefully examining and "getting to know" their apple. Guide them through the process. Have them look at size, shape, color variations, distinctive markings, etc. Make sure they look at the apple from all perspectives. You might even suggest they think of themselves as a spacecraft orbiting and studying their apple as if it were an asteroid or moon; or examining the apple as if it were a new life form never before found on Earth. They should pay careful attention to any characteristics that make their apple unique and different from all other apples. Soon they will have to pick it out of a crowd.

After students have studied their apples, collect them in the bowl. Unroll a section of paper on a table, and place all the apples on it. Then call students up to find and reclaim their apples, four to five students at a time. (The students will be surprised at how easy this is.)

Next, have each student write a clear, accurate and detailed description of his or her apple—one that will allow someone else to recognize it easily. If time allows, students should revise and write a final version of their description.

(If your class is larger than 10-12, divide into groups to complete the rest of this activity.)

Make enough numbered spaces on the paper for all the apples. Have students place their apples on one of the spaces when they finish their writing. (If possible, arrange your classroom so that other students won't see the apples as they are placed on the table.)

Once all the apples are on the table, have each student read his or her description. After each reading, everyone else should write down that student's name and the number of the apple they think has been described.

After everyone has had a chance to read, have each student identify his or her apple, and check to see how many others chose it correctly based on the description. The number of students that correctly identified each apple after listening to its description gives students feedback on how accurately their descriptions were written.

Now, students may eat their apples.

Monster Exchange
(Student Exercise D-1)

The instructions on the student worksheet should be self-explanatory. Emphasize the need to keep drawings and writings secret until the end of the activity. The success of their partners' drawings should provide students with feedback on the quality of their written instructions.

In place of step 5 on the student exercise, you may decide to collect all the descriptions, and then display the drawings on a bulletin board or tabletop. Read the descriptions and see if students can identify which drawings match each one.

Mystery Box
(Student Exercise D-2)

Instructions on the student worksheet should be self-explanatory.

Painting a Portrait in Writing
(Student Exercise D-3)

Distribute the student instruction sheet on page 97.

Emphasize the "no put-downs" rule. Remind students that they will have the right to strike anything from their partner's writing that they don't want the rest of the class to hear.

After students have completed their final drafts, collect them all and shuffle them. Then number each paragraph in the stack.

Have students number a piece of notebook paper with the number of students in the class.

Read each paragraph aloud. After you have finished each one, instruct students to write the name of the person they think it describes on their paper. As much as possible, limit discussion among the students as you do this. Important: If you notice words that might hurt someone's feelings, omit them.

Once you have read all the paragraphs, go back through the stack and tell the class who each paragraph was supposed to describe. As you identify each one, ask students to raise their hands if they identified the person correctly. This will provide feedback to the writers. The more people who raise their hands for a correct identification, the more thorough and accurate the descriptive writing must have been.

Through the Eyes of Another Species 1 and 2
(Student Exercises D-4 and D-5)

After students finish writing exercise D-4, your class may want to share by guessing which person each essay describes. Read the essays aloud, and have students write down the name of the person they think wrote each one. For exercise D-5 ask students to bring in pictures of their pets. Post all the pictures, take turns reading your descriptions and see if students can match each description with the right pet.

You Have to Get One of These . . .
(Student Exercise D-6)

Instructions on the student exercise should be self-explanatory. Use one of the "Writing Score Sheet" on page 134 to give students feedback.

Describing with Similes and Metaphors
(Student Exercise D-7)
Describing with Analogies
(Student Exercise D-8)

Instructions on the student worksheets should be self-explanatory.

Contrasting the Differences Between Two Things
(Student Exercise D-9)
Compare and Contrast
(Student Exercise D-10)

Instructions on the student exercises should be self-explanatory. You may choose to give feedback using the "Writing Score Sheet" on page 134.

Compare and contrast:
Macintosh and Windows computers
Two different fast-food restaurants (malls or department
    stores)
The U.S. Postal Service and e-mail
Two different musical groups
Salsa and ketchup, etc.

Imagine the perfect place for a vacation. Describe it in detail.

Imagine the ideal parent. Describe the qualities and behaviors that a parent should have. You might ask both students and parents to participate in this assignment, and then compare. The results could stimulate an interesting discussion.

Imagine an ideal school. What classes and activities would it have? How would instruction and discipline be handled? What would its physical plant look like? Describe a school that would be perfect for you.

Describe the most interesting or unusual weather you've ever experienced.

Describe your city or neighborhood to someone who has never been to this country.

Describe an embarrassing situation. Use details and active verbs to add humor, emotion and realism.

Student Exercise D-1

Monster Exchange

Step 1: On a separate sheet of plain paper, draw a monster. Let your imagination go wild! Make the monster as strange and unusual and fantastic as you can. This is TOP SECRET. Don't let anyone else see your drawing!

Step 2: Hide your drawing in your desk.

Step 3: On a separate sheet of lined paper, describe the monster you've drawn. Describe the monster completely. Include every detail, so that someone who has never seen this monster will know exactly what it looks like.

Step 4: Exchange the description you have written with someone else in your class. Read each other's description VERY carefully. Then on another plain sheet of paper, draw each other's monsters. Use ONLY the written descriptions to tell what the monsters look like. Do NOT talk to one another until you finish drawing.

Step 5: After everyone has finished his or her second drawing, take the hidden monsters out of the desks and compare. How close did you come? What does it mean if your partner's drawing looks like your original? It means you must have written a very good description!

Student Exercise D-2

Mystery Box

Choose any ordinary, household object. Write a complete description of the object, without naming it:

What is it made of?

____

____

Describe its shape, color and size.

____

____

____

How is it used?

____

____

____

Where would it ordinarily be found?

____

____

____

Turn the information above into a well-organized descriptive paragraph. Remember not to name the object.

After everyone is finished writing, each student should read his or her paragraph to the class. After each reader is finished, everyone else writes down what they think the object is. Once everyone is finished reading, go back and check. The more people who identify your object correctly, the better your descriptive writing must be.

96

Student Exercise D-3

Painting a Portrait in Writing

Choose a partner to work with. Your job will be to create a detailed portrait of your partner—in words. You'll describe his or her appearance and behavior as precisely and thoroughly as you can.

No put-downs are allowed!

Spend five minutes taking notes about your partner. Jot down words and phrases that describe his or her face, hair, eyes, mouth and other features. Also note the way this person speaks, stands, sits and moves.

Describe specific behaviors and actions of the person, rather than using general descriptors such as *brave, clever* or *loyal*.

Once you've collected your ideas, organize them into a detailed paragraph. Do not use the name of the person you are writing about anywhere in your paragraph. Other people will be guessing his or her identity later.

After you and your partner have completed your paragraphs, exchange papers. Suggest ways to make one another's paragraphs clearer and more descriptive.

Important: You have the right to delete anything in your partner's writing that you don't want the rest of the class to hear.

Return the paragraphs, and write final drafts to turn in.

Student Exercise D-4

Through the Eyes of Another Species 1

Imagine your pet could write about you. What would he or she say? You're going to write a description of yourself, through the eyes of your pet. (If you don't have a pet, imagine that you do. You can choose any type of pet you like.)

Remember the pet's point of view. Does it see you from knee level? If so, how will that affect how you appear?

What would your pet say you look like? Describe some of your physical characteristics.

____

____

What does your voice sound like? What kinds of things do you usually say?

____

____

What are your most common physical gestures (movements)? Don't forget to see these from the pet's point of view.

____

____

Describe some typical things you would do when you're with your pet.

____

____

How would your pet describe your personality?

____

____

How would your pet describe the way you treat him or her?

____

____

Use the ideas above to complete a descriptive essay about yourself, as seen through your pet's eyes.

Name _________________________________

Through the Eyes of Another Species 2

Now you're going to write about your pet. (If you don't have a pet, imagine that you do. You can choose any type of pet you like.) Make your description so precise and detailed that we'll be able to identify your pet from among a hundred different pets in a pet store.

What does your pet look like? Describe his or her physical characteristics.

____

____

What does your pet sound like?

____

Where would you be most likely to find your pet?

____

What are your pet's most common physical actions?

____

____

Describe some typical things your pet does.

____

____

What does your pet most like to eat?

____

Describe your pet's personality.

____

____

How does your pet respond to you and others?

____

____

Use the ideas above to complete a descriptive essay about your pet.

Student Exercise D-6

You Have to Get One of These . . .

Pick one of your favorite things—a video game, book, tool, toy or gadget. You get the idea.

What did you choose? ____

Describe the object. What does it look like? How big is it? What does it feel like? Be specific and detailed.

____

____

____

____

Describe what it does. Again, be specific and detailed.

____

____

____

____

Finally, explain to your readers why they too want to have one of these things. Explain why it is so valuable, useful or wonderful. Be convincing! Be insistent!

____

____

____

____

Turn these ideas into an essay describing your object. Convince the rest of the world that they want one, too.

Describing with Similes and Metaphors

Writers often use similes and metaphors to make their words more descriptive and vivid. Similes and metaphors are figures of speech—they create an image with language. Both compare one thing to another very different thing. Similes and metaphors add depth and beauty to writing.

What's the difference between a simile and a metaphor? A simile uses the words *like* or *as* to tell us that two very different things are similar. A metaphor compares by telling us that one thing *is* another, very different thing. For example:

Simile: His voice droned like a set of bagpipes, played badly.
Metaphor: His voice was a set of bagpipes, played badly.

Simile: The saplings were as graceful as dancers in the breeze.
Metaphor: The saplings were graceful dancers in the breeze.

Sometimes, the comparison in a metaphor can be implied rather than stated directly. This is known as a *submerged* metaphor. For example:

After the loss, their coach erupted. (Compares the coach to a volcano.)

Similes and metaphors can make your writing more beautiful and interesting. However, don't overdo it. These figures of speech should be used sparingly. Make your similes and metaphors original. Try to avoid trite phrases such as "pretty as a picture," or "slippery as an eel." Such overused expressions have lost their ability to describe in a fresh, creative way.

Now it's time to practice writing similes and metaphors. Choose any five of the subjects below. Write a sentence that uses a simile to describe each one. Then choose another five and write about them in sentences that use metaphors. Remember, your sentences should compare the subject to something very different.

face	eyes	ears	nose
muscles	feet	hair	skin
book	flower	computer	cloud
sky	forest	apple	lawn
street	city	moon	tiger
song	fog	house	office
teacher	principal	student	flag
telephone	shark	airplane	wave

Student Exercise D-8

Describing with Analogies

An analogy compares two different things that are similar in some way. It explains the similarity, as a way to describe one of the objects. Often, an analogy describes something abstract by comparing it to something more concrete and familiar.

Analogies and similes are very much alike. The difference is that a simile simply makes a comparison, while an analogy *explains* that comparison explicitly.

Here are some examples:

A computer is like a screwdriver. It's a tool that can make your work easier and more efficient.

An unsettled conflict is like a ticking bomb. You never know when it might explode.

Houseplants are like good friends. They brighten your home and bring it to life. And they know how to sit quietly and keep you company when you're blue.

Now it's your turn to write some analogies. Choose any five of the pairs of items below. On a separate sheet of paper, describe the first item in the pair by comparing to the second in an analogy.

painting—window

book—door

music—ocean

reading—vacation

conversation—forest

friendship—glue

plan—road map

knowledge—flashlight

brain—filing cabinet

idea—sunrise

love—apple

school—stew

city—book

friendship—garden

anger—thermostat

newspaper—telescope

Finally, create five more analogies on your own, about any subjects you choose.

Name ________________________

Contrasting the Differences Between Two Things

When you contrast two things, you describe their differences. In your school career, you will often be asked to contrast, or explain the differences between two different but similar things.

For example, here is a simplified list of the differences between cantaloupes and watermelons.

Cantaloupes	**Watermelons**
Have rough, tan-colored skin	Have smooth green skin
Have orange flesh	Have red flesh

Have small, pale seeds
        in a center cavity
	Have larger, black seeds
	        throughout the melon

When you organize a piece of writing that contrasts two things, you can do it in one of two ways. Start with a topic sentence. Then, contrast the different qualities one at a time, like this:

It's easy to tell the difference between a cantaloupe and a watermelon. A cantaloupe has rough, tan-colored skin, but a watermelon has smooth green skin. A cantaloupe has orange flesh on the inside while a watermelon has red flesh. A cantaloupe has small, pale seeds in a cavity at the center of the melon, while a watermelon has larger black seeds that are found throughout the flesh of the melon.

Or, you can talk about all the characteristics of one thing, and then contrast them with the characteristics of the other thing. But you must write about each set of characteristics in the same order. Here's an example:

It's easy to tell the difference between a cantaloupe and a watermelon. A cantaloupe has rough, tan-colored skin, and orange flesh on the inside. A cantaloupe also has small, pale seeds that grow in a cavity at the center of the melon. A watermelon has smooth green skin and red flesh. It has larger black seeds that are found throughout the flesh of the melon.

Now it's your turn to write paragraphs that contrast two different things. Here are some choices of things for you to contrast:

cats and dogs	chickens and ducks	spaghetti and macaroni
frogs and toads	SUVs and pickup trucks	dictionaries and encyclopedias
CDs and cassette tapes	CDs and MP3s	lemonade and cola
3.5" floppy discs and compact discs (CDs)		

Before you write your paragraphs, list at least three ways that your subjects differ.

Then, write two paragraphs, organized in the two different ways described above.

Student Exercise D-10

Compare and Contrast

One of the most common essay assignments you will get is to compare and contrast two similar things. When you *compare* two things, you describe their *similarities*. When you *contrast* two things, you describe their *differences*.

For example, here is a simple list of similarities and differences between gorillas and orangutans:

Similarities: Both live in the rain forest; both are herbivores; both are excellent climbers.

Differences: Gorillas live in Africa while orangutans live in Asia; gorillas are much larger than orangutans; gorillas live mostly on the ground while orangutans spend most of their time in the trees; gorillas live in social groups while adult orangutans live solitary lives.

One way to organize a piece of writing that compares and contrasts is to write about the similarities first, and then write about the differences. For example:

> The two largest species of ape are similar in some ways, and very different in others. Both gorillas and orangutans live in the rain forest. Gorillas and orangutans are both herbivores. They are both excellent climbers.
>
> However, gorillas are native to Africa, while orangutans live in Asia. Gorillas are much larger than their Asian cousins. Gorillas spend most of their time on the ground, while orangutans spend most of their time in the trees. Gorillas live in social groups, while adult orangutans live alone.

Another way to organize a piece of writing that compares and contrasts is to group the similarities together with their related differences. For example:

> The two largest species of ape are similar in some ways, and very different in others. Gorillas are much larger than orangutans. Both gorillas and orangutans are rain forest dwellers, but gorillas are native to Africa while orangutans live in Asia. Gorillas live in social groups, while adult orangutans live alone. Both gorillas and orangutans are herbivores. They are both excellent climbers, but gorillas spend most of their time on the ground, while orangutans spend most of their time in the trees.

Now it's your turn to write paragraphs that compare and contrast two different things. Here are some choices of things for you to write about:

zebras and horses	crocodiles and alligators	books and magazines
shovels and rakes	telescopes and microscopes	your town and New York City

Before you write your paragraphs, list at least three ways that the two things differ, and at least two ways that they are similar. Then, write two descriptions, organized in the two different ways shown above.

Letter Writing

Teacher Instructions

Students have lots of ideas and opinions on a variety of subjects. We want them to learn to express those opinions clearly and directly and support those opinions with reasons.

Letters make an ideal vehicle for practicing these skills. Good letters should be clearly reasoned, well-organized and to the point. But in the age of electronic communication, students may not respond well to letter writing activities if they see them as empty exercises. The activities in this section are intended to be more than just practice. We hope that students will actually use the letters they write to communicate their ideas to others.

As much as possible, encourage students to send or deliver the letters they write to the intended recipients. People write so that others will read their words. When students know that their letters will actually be read by the people they're addressed to, they will have a built-in motivation to write clearly and thoughtfully and to rewrite carefully. And when replies come back, or when a letter to the editor is printed in the local paper, the thrill that they experience will be an even greater motivator for additional writing.

Real letter writing also provides a built-in motivator for revising. Students will be more likely to get responses to their letters if they are clearly and neatly written, and error-free. Remind students that a good letter-writer CARES.

Student letters do get responses. Not all the time, of course, but often enough to make sending them worthwhile. Newspaper editors print letters from young people. Celebrities answer fan mail, or at least have it answered. Companies respond to complaints or compliments from their customers, even young ones, and most principals recognize the importance of responding to student concerns. Take advantage of all this willingness to respond to your young writers.

When students mail their requests for information, remind them that it's considered courteous to enclose a self-addressed, stamped envelope. This also increases the likelihood that they will receive a response.

A Letter to Your Principal
A Letter to a Company
A Letter to a Celebrity
A Letter to the Editor (Student Exercises
     L-1 through L-4)

Complete instructions can be found on the reproducible student worksheets. Use the "Letter Writing Evaluation Form" below and also found on page 140 to give students feedback.

Before students write letters to their principal, you may want to alert your administrator to expect them, and to ask for his or her support in responding to them. You may want to extend the same courtesy to the editor of your local paper.

Letter Writing Evaluation Form

____   _________________________________
Student author   Topic

_____ Begins with sentence(s) that explain the purpose of the letter.
[1-5]

_____ Viewpoint/request of the writer is clearly stated.
[1-5]

_____ Includes reasons, details, and/or examples.
[1-5]

_____ Follows correct letter format—includes heading, greeting, body, closing, signature and
[1-5]   inside address (business letters only).

_____ Spelling/Punctuation/Capitalization are correct. (Subtract one point for each error.)
[0-5]

_____ Grammar is correct. (Subtract one point for each error.)
[0-5]

_____ Looks like a final product: neat and legible.
[1-5]

Ask Quizelda
(Student Exercise L-5)

This activity is one that students can do for fun. Allow students to share some of their questions and responses after their writing is completed. No additional evaluation is required.

Writing E-mails
(Student Exercise L-6)

Directions for this activity should be self-explanatory. If possible, allow students to send their e-mail messages, and e-mail them to you for evaluation as well.

A Letter to the Future
(Student Exercises L-7A and L-7B)

Directions for these activities should be self-explanatory. Give students the choice of doing one or the other of these assignments. Use the "Letter Writing Evaluation Form" on page 140 to give students feedback.

A Letter of Appreciation
(Student Exercise L-8)

Directions for this activity should be self-explanatory. Encourage your students to deliver their letters to the people they write about.

Additional Letter Writing Prompts
Friendly Letters

Write a letter of condolence (also called a sympathy letter) to a friend whose grandparent has died. Include any personal memories you may have of happy times spent with this friend's grandparent.

Write a letter inviting a friend to a family cookout. Make sure to tell about some of the events that are planned for the day.

Write a letter to someone in a foreign country, telling him or her about our educational system.

Write a letter to a relative who lives in another state, and who is thinking of moving to your hometown. Tell him or her about the advantages and disadvantages of living here.

Write a letter of application for a summer job as
    a. a baby-sitter
    b. a lifeguard
    c. a camp counselor
    d. a teacher's aide
    e. a museum volunteer
    f. a store clerk
    g. other

Write a letter of application to a special summer program offered to students in your school district. In your letter, explain why you are interested in the subject, and describe activities in which you have participated that would qualify you to be selected.

Write a letter of recommendation or nomination for a special award such as the Teacher of the Year Award.

Write a letter to the Superintendent of Schools or the Chairman of the School Board requesting funds for:
    a. school renovation
    b. air conditioning
    c. an elevator for your school
    d. after school programs
    e. extended day programs
    f. food service improvement

Write a letter to the Superintendent of Schools or the Chairman of the School Board commending an employee at your school for their good work. Be specific and detailed in your description of what they have done well.

Write a letter to the mayor, governor, city council member, delegate or state senator thanking them for __________, or requesting them to support ____________.

Write a letter to your congressional representative, senator or President, requesting that they take a particular position on an issue (school funding, racial profiling, homelessness or medical research, for example).

Write a letter to the editor of your local newspaper:

    a. praising school staff, peer mediators, police, firemen, etc., for jobs well done.

    b. praising one of your school's sports or scholastic problem-solving teams for excellence in competition, winning, losing gracefully, etc.

    c. expressing your opinion regarding:

        1. dress codes
        2. gun control
        3. death penalty
        4. teen recreation
        5. animal rights
        6. juvenile justice
        7. TV violence
        8. music censorship
        9. public transportation
       10. responses to an article or other letter printed in the paper.

Write a letter to the tourism office of a state or city of your choice. Ask for information about tourist attractions, restaurants, accommodations, etc.

Student Exercise L-1

Expressing Your Opinion
A Letter to the Principal

Your school is perfect, right? Of course it's not! No matter how good it is, everything can stand some improvement. So, make a list of some changes that your school could make to become better.

____

____

____

Go back and look at your list. Choose one thing that would really make a difference and could realistically be changed or improved. Try to select something that will benefit many students.

____

____

Explain why you think this change is needed.

____

____

____

Explain, in detail, exactly what you think should be done to make this change or improvement.

____

____

____

Finally, write these ideas in the form of a letter to your principal or school board member. Make sure your reasons are clearly stated. Don't forget to follow the proper form for letter writing, and sign your letter. If you're not certain about the correct form of a business letter, check in your English textbook or some other style manual.

This is a real letter. After the letter has been checked by your teacher, it will actually be delivered to the principal.

Name ______________________________

Expressing Your Opinion
A Letter to a Company

Do you have a favorite breakfast cereal, soft drink, cookie, toy or brand of clothing? Make a list of the products you like best.

____

____

Look at your list and pick one product that you would like to write a letter about.

____

What's special about this product? Why do you like it so much?

____

____

When do you use this product?

____

Why do you like this particular brand, rather than other similar products from other companies?

____

____

Make a suggestion that would make this product even better.

____

____

Use these ideas to write a letter to the company that makes your favorite product. Address your letter to the Customer Relations Director (the person who communicates with customers who have complaints or comments). Make sure to follow the proper form for writing a business letter.

The company's address is usually printed on the product's packaging. If not, you can probably find it on the internet. After your teacher has checked your work, mail your letter. Include a self-addressed stamped envelope. You may get an answer!

Student Exercise L-3

A Letter to a Celebrity

Which TV stars, musicians, authors, movie actors and other celebrities do you like best? Make a list of some of your favorites.

____

____

____

Go back and look at your list. Choose one person to whom you would like to write a letter.

____

Explain why you chose this person. What's special about him or her? As much as possible, focus on career achievements rather than physical qualities.

____

____

What has this person done that you've especially liked? What did you like about it?

____

____

____

What are your special wishes or hopes for this person's career in the future?

____

____

____

Now write a letter to your favorite celebrity that tells him or her what you've said above. Make sure to follow the proper form for writing a friendly letter.

You will probably be able to find an address for your celebrity on the internet. After your teacher has checked your letter, why not mail it, or e-mail it? Celebrities often answer their mail. You may get a letter back. Don't forget to include a self-addressed stamped envelope.

Student Exercise L-4

A Letter to the Editor

Letters to the editor are some of the most widely read words in the newspaper. Here's how to write a good one that might be chosen for publication:

✎ Write in response to a story or another letter that appeared in the paper recently. Refer to that story in the first sentence or two of your letter.

✎ Stick to a single issue. State your point clearly, simply and directly.

✎ Support your point with a few short reasons and examples. Editors will be most interested in letters that offer new information or express a clear opinion on an issue the newspaper has covered.

✎ Sign your name, and give an address and telephone number so that the editor can verify that you actually wrote the letter. Remember, if your letter is published, your name will appear with it, so think and write carefully.

✎ Keep it short and simple. Space is precious to newspaper editors. They would rather print three short letters than one long, rambling one. Sometimes editors may shorten your letter even further before they print it.

Here's a sample:

Editor of the Editorial Pages
Richmond Times-Leader
Box 100
Richmond, VA 55555
May 14, 2002

Editor, Times-Leader:

Yesterday's paper carried a story about Councilwoman Gloria Holloway's efforts to bring a community center to her Southside district. As a resident of that district, I fully support this project. We currently have no recreation center in our community. Children in our neighborhood need a safe, well-maintained place where they can participate in organized sports, get homework help, do arts and crafts and spend time with other young people in a supervised setting. Such a facility would also benefit adults in our community. A new community center will make our neighborhood, and our city a better place to live.

Sincerely,
Ima Citizen
2007 Washington Ave.
Richmond, VA 55555
(804) 555-5555

Now it's your turn. Find an article or letter in the newspaper, and write your response in the form of a letter to the editor.

114

Student Exercise L-5

Ask Quizelda

Quizelda writes an advice column in the local newspaper. Here's an example;

> Dear Quizelda,
> I think I'm old enough to take care of myself. But my parents still won't let me stay home
> alone. How can I convince them that I'm ready to be left at home without a baby-sitter?
> Mr. Responsible
>
> Dear Mr. Responsible,
> You may think you are grown up and responsible, but you still have to convince your parents.
> Why don't you . . .

Sometimes Quizelda's answers are funny. Sometimes they're serious. But they're always interesting and carefully written.

Quizelda is planning to take a short vacation. The newspaper needs someone to write her column while she is away. First, write two interesting questions for Quizelda to answer. Your questions can ask about imaginary problems, or real ones.

Dear Quizelda,

____

____

____

____

Signed, ___________________________

Dear Quizelda,

____

____

____

____

Signed, ___________________________

Now, exchange papers with a classmate. On a separate sheet of paper, write Quizelda's answers.

Student Exercise L-6

Writing E-mails

Electronic mail (e-mail) is a useful and convenient way to communicate in our modern world. It's the most widely used feature of the internet. Unfortunately, people often become careless or sloppy when they send e-mail. Most of the rules of good English and good etiquette that apply to ordinary letters also apply to e-mail messages.

Here are some tips for writing good e-mail messages.

✎ Don't forget to fill in the subject line at the top of the message, so the recipient will know what your e-mail is about.

✎ Always sign your messages. Your internet log-on might not tell others who you are. People may also include a postal address and phone number as part of their signature. WARNING: Do not give your address or phone number to strangers you meet in chat rooms or other individuals whose identity you are not certain about.

✎ E-mails can be shorter and more informal than handwritten or typed letters. But they should still be written in standard English.

✎ Check your grammar and spelling. Because e-mail is so quick and easy, people often neglect to correct simple errors. This can make a bad impression on the recipient.

✎ Use emoticons [text symbols to express feelings, such as ;) or : ( ] only in friendly correspondence. They are not appropriate for business e-mails.

✎ Remember that your message will be read by another person. Follow the golden rule—treat that person as you would like to be treated yourself.

Here are several ideas for e-mails you can write. Choose any two, and write them on a separate sheet of paper (or on a computer, of course):

A request for information about where to purchase a product.

An invitation to a friend to go with your family to a nearby amusement park.

A letter to your congressperson or senator about a current issue.

A note to a friend telling about what you did over the weekend.

An invitation to a college professor to speak to your class.

A request to a television station to broadcast a local sports event.

A message to a relative in another part of the country that shares family news.

Student Exercise L-7A

A Letter to the Future

What do you imagine the future holds for you? What are your goals, plans and dreams? For this assignment, you'll write a letter to yourself, 25 years from now.

What do you hope you'll accomplish in your education?

____

____

What are your career goals?

____

____

What hobbies and interests do you plan to pursue?

____

____

What do you think your personal and family life will be like?

____

____

What plans do you have for travel and adventure?

____

____

What advice do you have for the middle-aged you?

____

____

Put all these ideas into a letter addressed to yourself, 25 years in the future.

Student Exercise L-7B

A Letter to the Future

Think about how different life is now than it was just 50 or 100 years ago. Now think back even far-ther—1000 years ago. People from that time would recognize almost nothing in our modern world. For this assignment, you'll write a letter to the people of the future, 1000 years from now. Remember, language and culture change over time. You can't just name things (like computers or CDs, for example.) You'll have to describe things and clearly explain their purpose.

Describe what your home is like.

____

____

____

____

Describe your community.

____

____

____

____

Describe our system of government.

____

____

____

____

Describe our educational system.

____

____

____

____

Student Exercise L-7B

A Letter to the Future *continued*

Describe some of the most recent developments in technology.

____

____

____

____

____

Discuss the current problems facing the human race.

____

____

____

____

Discuss some of the important lessons the human race has learned that you would most like people of the future to know.

____

____

____

____

Put all these ideas into a letter addressed to our descendants, 1000 years into the future.

Student Exercise L-8

A Letter of Appreciation

Every one of us has a former teacher, principal or other adult mentor who has made a difference in our lives. Those people deserve our thanks. Write a letter that tells this person how much you appreciate them.

Who is the person you'd like to thank?

____

What is/was that person's position?

____

What makes this person special to you? Be specific.

____

____

How did he or she affect your life?

____

____

Think of one (or more) specific events when this person helped you. Describe the event(s).

____

____

____

What have you learned about life, or about yourself from this person?

____

____

____

Use the information you've gathered above to write a letter to this special person. Tell how he or she has changed your life, and thank them for their efforts. Make sure you revise before you write your final draft.

Writing for Speaking
Teacher Instructions

The activities in this section will give students practice in both writing and speaking. They may also be used when students need a break from some of the more demanding, academically oriented activities in *21st Century Writing*. They are not intended as a series of consecutive lessons; nor do they have to be presented in any particular order. Use them with your class when the time seems right.

Some students may feel uncomfortable speaking before an audience. Encourage students to participate in that part of the activity, but allow them to opt out if they choose. For many students, having a written plan prepared in advance will help them feel more relaxed as they speak.

For those students who are willing, try videotaping their talks. Viewing these tapes can be tremendously useful as students work to improve the quality of their presentations. Play back the video to give them direct feedback without their having to hear—and perhaps defend themselves from—critical comments from peers. You may even want to send the tapes home so parents can see what their children have accomplished in class.

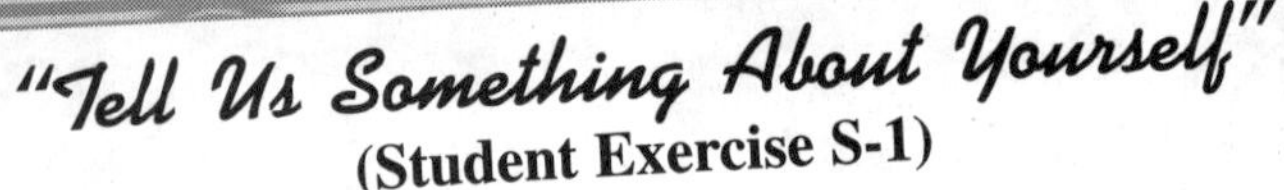

"Tell Us Something About Yourself"
(Student Exercise S-1)

Instructions on the student exercise should be self-explanatory. After students speak, they should give one another feedback using the "Public Speaking Evaluation Form" on page 142.

Retelling a Folktale or Fairy Tale
(no student worksheet)

Almost everyone knows the story of Little Red Riding Hood, or the Three Little Pigs. We all know folktales and fairy tales from childhood. But knowing a story and telling a story are two different things. This activity will give students a chance to develop their storytelling skills.

First have students write out a folk or fairy tale—exactly as they would tell it. Then have them pair up, read their tale aloud to a partner and make whatever revisions are necessary.

Finally, have them tell their story to the class. Have students use the "Public Speaking Evaluation Form" on page 142 to give each speaker feedback on their performance.

Class Clown: Telling a Joke
(Student Exercise S-2)

Instructions on the student exercise should be self-explanatory. Use of the "Public Speaking Evaluation Form" on page 142 is optional for this activity.

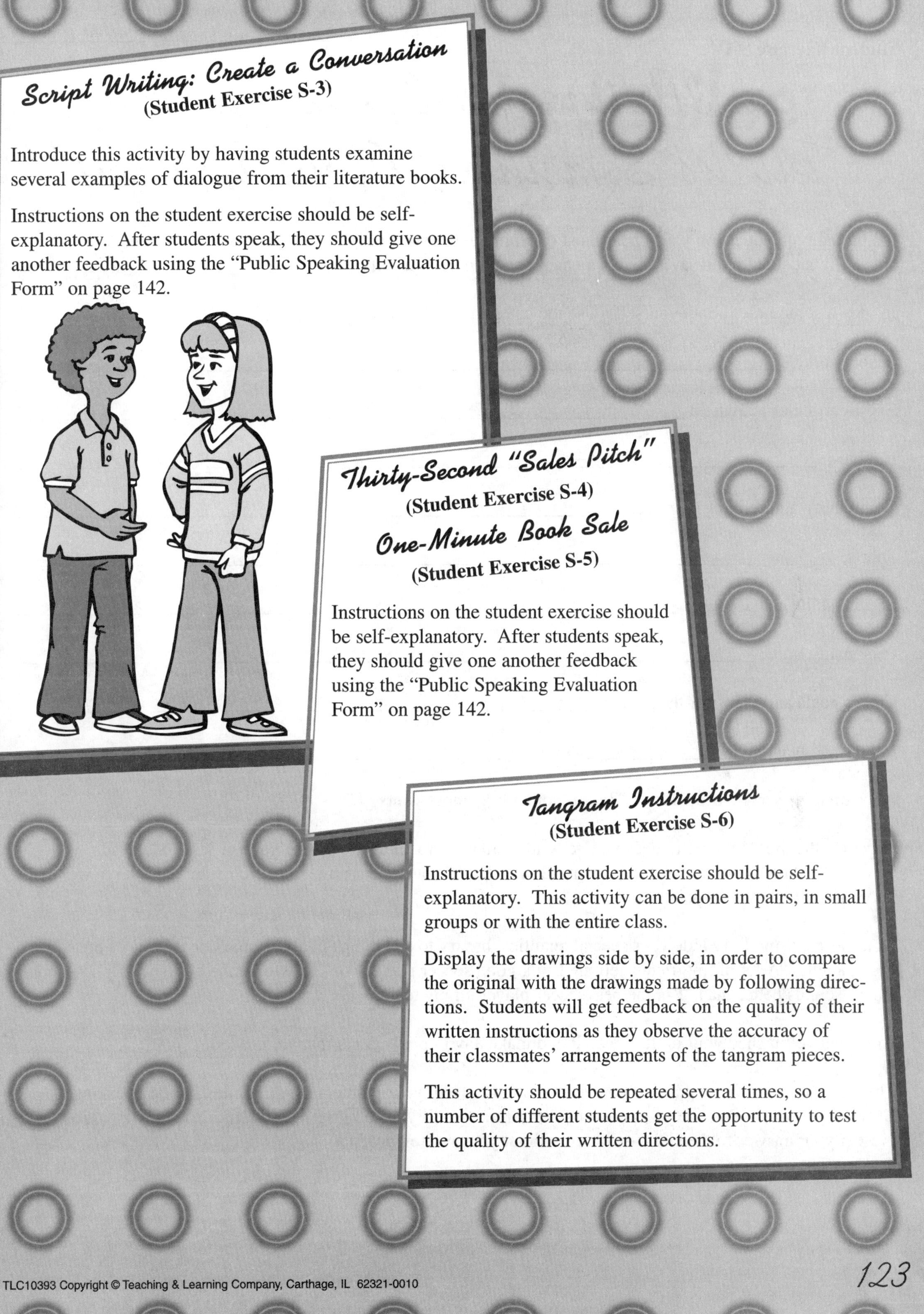

Script Writing: Create a Conversation
(Student Exercise S-3)

Introduce this activity by having students examine several examples of dialogue from their literature books.

Instructions on the student exercise should be self-explanatory. After students speak, they should give one another feedback using the "Public Speaking Evaluation Form" on page 142.

Thirty-Second "Sales Pitch"
(Student Exercise S-4)
One-Minute Book Sale
(Student Exercise S-5)

Instructions on the student exercise should be self-explanatory. After students speak, they should give one another feedback using the "Public Speaking Evaluation Form" on page 142.

Tangram Instructions
(Student Exercise S-6)

Instructions on the student exercise should be self-explanatory. This activity can be done in pairs, in small groups or with the entire class.

Display the drawings side by side, in order to compare the original with the drawings made by following directions. Students will get feedback on the quality of their written instructions as they observe the accuracy of their classmates' arrangements of the tangram pieces.

This activity should be repeated several times, so a number of different students get the opportunity to test the quality of their written directions.

Name ________________________

Writing for Speaking: "Tell Us Something About Yourself"

It's probably the question you'll hear most often in interviews for high school or a job. It's a simple question, but . . . What should you say? Here's a chance to prepare yourself.

Jot down some notes about yourself. Use the categories below.

Schoolwork: ____

Extra-curricular activities: ___________________________________

Hobbies: ____

Community and religious service: ______________________________

Sports: ____

Special skills and abilities: ___________________________________

Personality traits: ____

Career goals and plans for the future: __________________________

Values and beliefs: ____

Now, imagine you've been asked, "Tell us something about yourself."

Organize the most important ideas you've written above into an answer—one page or less. Make sure you include the things that are most important. Be honest, of course, but remember, you want the interviewer to know about your strong points.

Don't let your modesty hide your special qualities, but try to say things in a way that doesn't sound boastful. For example, "A lot of my friends tell me I'm a good soccer player," or "I try to be the best soccer player possible," sounds better than "I'm the best soccer player on my team."

After you've finished your draft, reread it and make any improvements that are needed.

Then, in groups of three, practice your answer aloud. Help your partners by using the "Public Speaking Evaluation Form." Practice your answer several times, until you can give it smoothly. You may be asked to present your answer to the class—with or without your written product.

124

Student Exercise S-2

Class Clown: Telling a Joke

Do you know the difference between a joke and a riddle? A riddle is a question with a clever or funny answer. A joke is a funny story. Jokes are usually longer than riddles. Here's an example of each:

Here's a famous riddle, the Riddle of the Sphinx:
> What walks on four legs in the morning, two legs at noon and three legs in the evening?
> (Answer below.)

And here's a joke:
> A biologist was delivering a flock of penguins to the zoo. On the way, his truck broke down. He was desperate to deliver the penguins, so he waved down a passing car.
> "Listen," he told the driver. "I'll give you 50 dollars if you take these penguins to the zoo."
> The motorist thought about it for a moment.
> "Okay, I'll give you a hundred dollars," the biologist said.
> "It's a deal," the man said. He loaded the penguins into his car and drove away.
> A few hours later, after his truck was fixed, the biologist drove to the zoo to make sure the penguins had gotten there safely. They weren't there! The biologist was frantic. He drove all around the city, looking for the man and his penguins.
> Finally he saw them walking down the street. The man was carrying a box of popcorn.
> "Hey!" the biologist yelled. "I gave you a hundred bucks to take those penguins to the zoo!"
> "I did take them to the zoo," the man answered. "But we still had some money left over, so we decided to go to the movies, too."

Now, here's your assignment:
Find three good riddles, and one good joke. All must be appropriate for school. Use good judgement. If you don't know any good jokes or riddles, there should be plenty of books in the library to help you find some.
Write the riddles and joke, exactly as you would tell them. Practice telling them aloud at home. Use a strong, expressive voice.
As you read your joke and riddles, revise what you've written so it's clear and understandable, and sounds funny.

Finally, you will have a chance to tell your joke and riddles to the class. Try not to give them away ahead of time.

Answer: Man (crawls as a baby, walks on two legs as an adult and walks with a cane in old age.)

Student Exercise S-3

Script Writing: Create a Conversation

Let's write a conversation for two people to present. You'll write it in the form of a script, like a short play.

Here's a short example:
Shakita: Mom, what's for dinner?
Mrs. Venable: Carrot casserole with tofu chunks. Your favorite!
Shakita: Again! But we had that yesterday.
Mrs. Venable: I know. But you liked it so much I decided to heat up the leftovers for tonight.
Shakita: Oh, great! Leftover carrot goo.
Mrs. Venable: Don't get smart, young lady! Lots of children would love to have some of Mrs. Venable's famous carrot casserole.
Shakita: I know, Mom. Sorry.
Mrs. Venable: Go wash up. Dinner's in five minutes.

Try to make your script sound like an actual conversation. Remember, people don't always speak in complete sentences. Sometimes they interrupt one another. Use partial sentences and phrases to make the dialogue sound real.

Here's an exercise for practice. Write a conversation between two imaginary people about one of the following topics:

✎Which singing group they like the best.

✎Which basketball star (or football star, etc.) is the best athlete.

✎What is their favorite food, or their favorite place to eat.

✎Where they plan to go to high school.

✎Or, choose another topic instead.

Your script should have at least five different sentences for each speaker. After you've finished writing, find a partner and read your dialogue aloud. Do the words sound realistic?

Revise your writing to make it sound like two real people talking to one another. Then, produce a final copy of your script. When everyone is ready, perform your conversation for the class.

Student Exercise S-4

Thirty-Second "Sales Pitch"

For this activity, your challenge is to convince classmates that they should try one of your favorite things. And you have 30 seconds to do it.

First, make a list of some of your favorite things: books, foods, movies, musical performers, restaurants, games and so on.

____

____

____

Circle the one you'd most like to speak about.

Write down as many wonderful things about your choice as you can think of.

____

____

____

____

____

____

Now, write your "sales pitch." Convince other people that they too should try this favorite thing of yours. Your speech can't last longer than 30 seconds.

After you have written your speech, practice with a partner. Time one another to make sure your speeches aren't too long. Revise your speech to make it even more convincing.

Finally, you'll have the chance to present your sales pitch to the entire class, and get feedback from the "Public Speaking Evaluation Form."

127

Name _______________________

One-Minute Book Sale

For this activity, your challenge is to convince classmates that they should read a book you like. You have exactly one minute to convince them.

First, which book are you going to "sell"?

____

Who is the author?

____

What is the book about? Give a quick plot summary.

____

____

____

Who are the most interesting characters?

____

____

____

Why should someone want to read this book?

____

____

____

Now, write your "sales pitch." Convince other people that they want to read this book. Your speech can't last longer than one minute. Be creative. You might want to speak as one of the characters in the story. Or you could present your pitch as a news reporter, or a literary salesman. Or speak as if you were the book itself.

After you have written your speech, practice with a partner. Time one another to make sure your speeches aren't too long. Revise your speech to make it even more convincing.

Finally, you'll have a chance to present your speech to the entire class, and get feedback from the "Public Speaking Evaluation Form."

Student Exercise S-6

Tangram Instructions

A set of tangram pieces is printed below. Carefully cut them apart. Then arrange them into a design or pattern of your own choice. Don't let anyone else see your design.

After you are satisfied with your design, make a drawing of the pattern you have created on the next page (page 130).

Next, write a set of directions on page 131 that tells classmates exactly how to re-create your design. Make sure the instructions are precise and orderly. After you finish writing, you'll have a chance to read your directions to other students. Then you'll compare their creations with your drawing. That should tell you if your directions were accurate enough for them to follow.

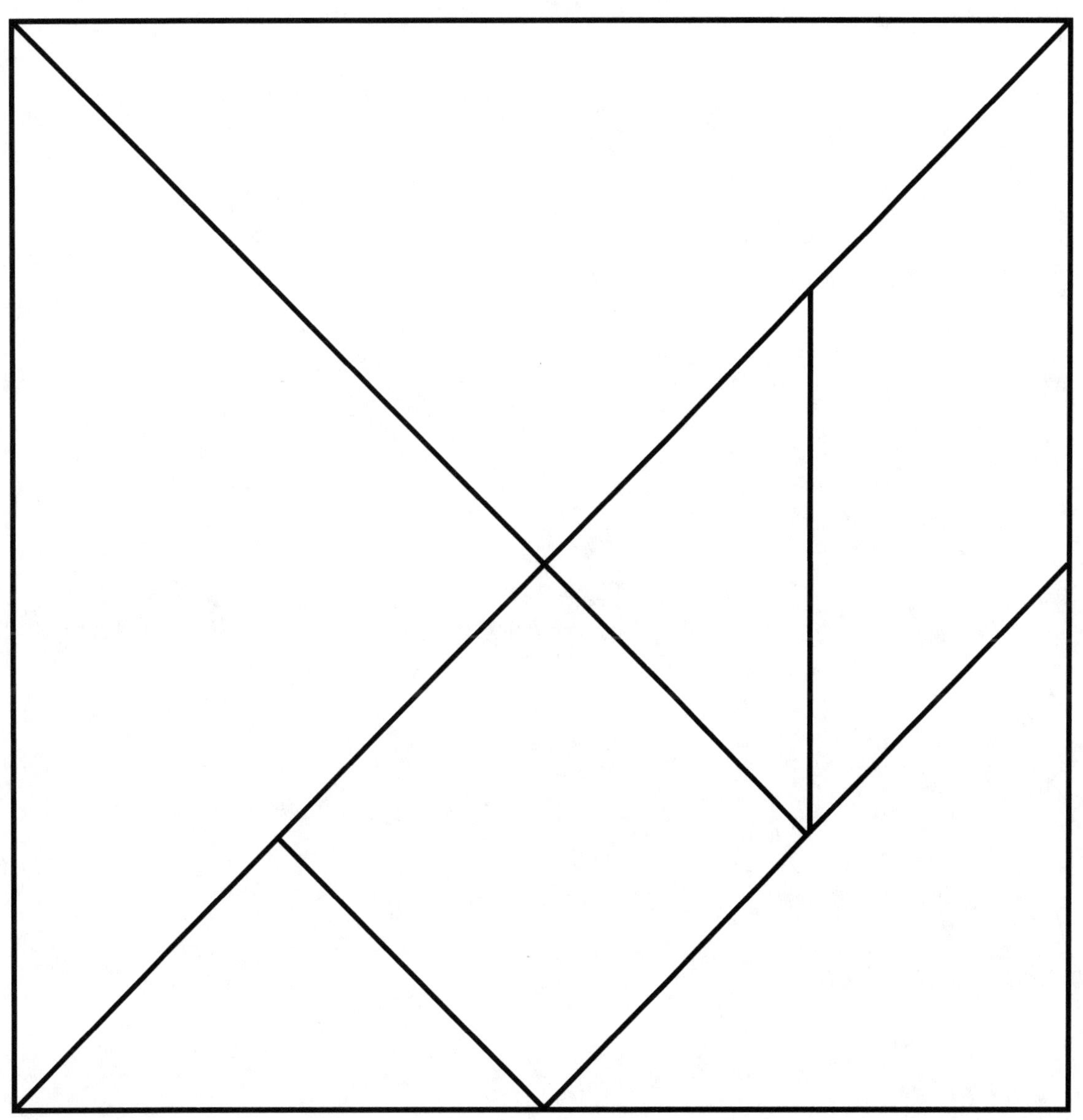

Name _______________________________

My Tangram

Student Exercise S-6

My Tangram Instructions

Write a set of directions that tells classmates exactly how to re-create your design. Make sure the instructions are precise and orderly. After you finish writing, you'll have a chance to read your directions to other students. Then you'll compare their creations with your drawing. That should tell you if your directions were accurate enough for them to follow.

Grading rubrics are effective tools for assessing student work. They will also help students improve their writing skills.

It can be difficult to judge student writing. But a rubric provides objective criteria for evaluation. Using a rubric allows a teacher to know exactly what to look for when assessing students' work. No more "holistic" scoring. No more mystified students wondering why they received a particular grade.

Give students the rubric you will use to evaluate them *before* they do the assignment. Then they will know what you are looking for ahead of time, and can focus on those aspects of writing as they work.

At first, using rubrics may seem to take more time. But as you become familiar with the assessment categories and scoring options, evaluation becomes faster, more efficient and much more effective.

Remember to write comments on your students' papers, as well as scoring them with the rubric. These comments will let students know that you have read their work carefully, and value their efforts.

There may be times when the sample rubrics in this appendix will be too complex or all-inclusive for your purposes. If your students need work on a particular aspect of their writing (composing or usage and mechanics, for example), tell them ahead of time that you will assess them on only that aspect of their work. Use only that portion of the score sheet or rubric, and disregard the rest (or offer bonus points for exceptional work in the other areas).

Rubrics also give students a guide to follow as they work to improve their writing. Again, we strongly recommend that students be allowed to revise and resubmit writing assignments for a second evaluation. This will encourage them to examine your assessment and continue working to make their writing better and better.

The first two score sheets are designed to be used with writing assignments of all sorts. They allow teachers to grade on a 100-point scale. The two charts that follow present the same group of criteria, but allow teachers the alternative of discriminating among four levels of achievement—excellent, good, needs improvement and weak. The remaining score sheets and rubrics are designed for specific types of writing assignments found in various sections of the book.

Students can also use these pages for peer evaluations. When you allow students to assist one another with peer evaluations, it's a good idea to have student writers evaluate themselves using the same rubric, and then compare their own evaluation with that of their partner.

And of course, we encourage you to create your own rubrics—ones that will meet your students' needs as developing writers, and your own needs as a teacher.

Writing Evaluation

Composing

______ Has a clear central idea or topic.
(1-10)

______ Elaborated with supporting details and specific examples.
(1-10)

______ Logically organized; has an orderly structure.
(1-5)

______ Maintains unity; stays on topic; uses effective opening and closing.
(1-5)

Expression

______ Uses appropriate, interesting vocabulary.
(1-5)

______ Uses appropriate tone; word choices reflect writer's viewpoint.
(1-5)

______ Displays author's voice; writer's personality is evident.
(1-5)

______ Uses a variety of sentence lengths and types.
(1-5)

Usage/Mechanics (Subtract one point for each error.)

______ Uses standard word order and complete sentences.
(0-5)

______ Uses correct word meanings, verb tense, subject/verb agreement and parts of speech.
(0-5)

______ Uses correct capitalization, punctuation, paragraphing and spelling.
(0-10)

General

______ Shows evidence of revision/rewriting
(10)

______ Neatly and carefully written or typed
(10)

______ On Time   ______ Total
(10)

Format based on Virginia Standards of Learning.

Student ________________________________

(100 maximum)

Writing Score Sheet

______ **Composition**
Well-organized with beginning, middle and end; follows a logical order; has central idea supported with details, reasons and examples; maintains unity. (30 pts.)

______ **Style**
Uses well-chosen vocabulary; uses effective images and figures of speech; uses appropriate tone and voice; revised for clarity. (20 possible)

______ **Sentence Structure**
Uses standard word order and complete sentences; avoids run-on sentences and sentence fragments; uses varied sentence length and type. (10 pts.)

______ **Usage**
Uses words, verb tense, plurals, word endings and parts of speech correctly. (10 pts.)

______ **Mechanics**
Correct capitalization, punctuation, paragraphing and spelling. (10 pts.)

______ **Neatly and Carefully Completed and on Time** (20 pts.)

Student ________________________________

(100 maximum)

Writing Score Sheet

______ **Composition**
Well-organized with beginning, middle and end; follows a logical order; has central idea supported with details, reasons and examples; maintains unity. (30 pts.)

______ **Style**
Uses well-chosen vocabulary; uses effective images and figures of speech; uses appropriate tone and voice; revised for clarity. (20 possible)

______ **Sentence Structure**
Uses standard word order and complete sentences; avoids run-on sentences and sentence fragments; uses varied sentence length and type. (10 pts.)

______ **Usage**
Uses words, verb tense, plurals, word endings and parts of speech correctly. (10 pts.)

______ **Mechanics**
Correct capitalization, punctuation, paragraphing and spelling. (10 pts.)

______ **Neatly and Carefully Completed and on Time** (20 pts.)

Format based on Virginia Literacy Passport.

Writing Assessment

	Excellent	Good	Needs Improvement	Weak
Content: Has a clear main idea and interesting information; uses supporting details; stays on subject.				
Organization: Has beginning, middle and end; gives reasons and examples; follows logical order.				
Tone and Voice: Shows writer's feelings and personality.				
Vocabulary: Uses.grammatically correct, specific, precise word choice; uses colorful, descriptive language.				
Sentences: Uses clear, complete sentences; varies sentence types and lengths; writing flows smoothly.				
Mechanics: Correct spelling, punctuation and paragraphing; neatly and carefully completed.				

Student ______________________________

Writing Assessment

	Excellent	Good	Needs Improvement	Weak
Content: Has a clear main idea and interesting information; uses supporting details; stays on subject.				
Organization: Has beginning, middle and end; gives reasons and examples; follows logical order.				
Tone and Voice: Shows writer's feelings and personality.				
Vocabulary: Uses.grammatically correct, specific, precise word choice; uses colorful, descriptive language.				
Sentences: Uses clear, complete sentences; varies sentence types and lengths; writing flows smoothly.				
Mechanics: Correct spelling, punctuation and paragraphing; neatly and carefully completed.				

Writing Assessment

Composing	Excellent	Good	Needs Improvement	Weak
Has a clear central idea or topic.				
Elaborated with supporting details and specific examples.				
Logically organized; has an orderly structure.				
Maintains unity; stays on topic; uses effective opening and closing.				

Expression	Excellent	Good	Needs Improvement	Weak
Uses appropriate, interesting vocabulary.				
Uses appropriate tone; word choices reflect writer's viewpoint.				
Displays author's voice; writer's personality is evident.				
Uses a variety of sentence lengths and types.				

Usage/Mechanics	Excellent	Good	Needs Improvement	Weak
Uses standard word order and complete sentences.				
Uses correct word meanings, verb tense, subject/verb agreement and parts of speech.				
Uses correct capitalization, punctuation, paragraphing and spelling.				
Neatly and carefully written or typed.				

Format based on Virginia Standards of Learning.

Personal Essay Evaluation Form

____   _________________________________

Student author   Topic

_______ Begins with a sentence that introduces the topic.
[1-5]

_______ Presents at least two reasons to support the topic sentence.
[1-5]

_______ Provides specific details and examples in support of each reason.
[1-10]

_______ Information is presented in a logical order.
[1-5]

_______ Spelling is correct. (Subtract one point for each error.)
[0-5]

_______ Punctuation/capitalization is correct. (Subtract one point for each error.)
[0-5]

_______ Grammar and usage is correct. (Subtract one point for each error.)
[0-5]

_______ Looks like a final product: neat and legible.
[1-10]

____
Total (50 maximum)

Comments:

____

____

____

____

____

Writing Directions Score Sheet

_________________________________   _________________________________
Student author   Topic

_______ Directions are complete and detailed (include all necessary information).
[1-10]

_______ Directions are presented in order.
[1-5]

_______ No unnecessary information is included.
[1-5]

_______ Spelling is correct. (Subtract one point for each error.)
[0-5]

_______ Grammar is correct. (Subtract one point for each error.)
[0-5]

_______ Looks like a final product: neat and legible.
[1-5]

Writing Directions Score Sheet

_________________________________   _________________________________
Student author   Topic

_______ Directions are complete and detailed (include all necessary information).
[1-10]

_______ Directions are presented in order.
[1-5]

_______ No unnecessary information is included.
[1-5]

_______ Spelling is correct. (Subtract one point for each error.)
[0-5]

_______ Grammar is correct. (Subtract one point for each error.)
[0-5]

_______ Looks like a final product: neat and legible.
[1-5]

Technical/Expository Writing Evaluation Form

____   _________________________________

Student author   Topic

_____ Begins with a sentence that introduces the topic.
[1-5]

_____ Information is complete (includes all the information given).
[1-5]

_____ Information is presented in a logical order.
[1-5]

_____ Spelling/Punctuation/Capitalization are correct. (Subtract one point for each error.)
[0-5]

_____ Grammar is correct. (Subtract one point for each error.)
[0-5]

_____ Looks like a final product: neat and legible.
[1-5]

Technical/Expository Writing Evaluation Form

____   _________________________________

Student author   Topic

_____ Begins with a sentence that introduces the topic.
[1-5]

_____ Information is complete (includes all the information given).
[1-5]

_____ Information is presented in a logical order.
[1-5]

_____ Spelling/Punctuation/Capitalization are correct. (Subtract one point for each error.)
[0-5]

_____ Grammar is correct. (Subtract one point for each error.)
[0-5]

_____ Looks like a final product: neat and legible.
[1-5]

Letter Writing Evaluation Form

______________________________   ______________________________

Student author   Topic

______ Begins with sentence(s) that explain the purpose of the letter.
[1-5]

______ Viewpoint/request of the writer is clearly stated.
[1-5]

______ Includes reasons, details, and/or examples.
[1-5]

______ Follows correct letter format—includes heading, greeting, body, closing, signature and
[1-5] inside address (business letters only).

______ Spelling/Punctuation/Capitalization are correct. (Subtract one point for each error.)
[0-5]

______ Grammar is correct. (Subtract one point for each error.)
[0-5]

______ Looks like a final product: neat and legible.
[1-5]

Letter Writing Evaluation Form

______________________________   ______________________________

Student author   Topic

______ Begins with sentence(s) that explain the purpose of the letter.
[1-5]

______ Viewpoint/request of the writer is clearly stated.
[1-5]

______ Includes reasons, details, and/or examples.
[1-5]

______ Follows correct letter format— includes heading, greeting, body, closing, signature and
[1-5] inside address (business letters only).

______ Spelling/Punctuation/Capitalization are correct. (Subtract one point for each error.)
[0-5]

______ Grammar is correct. (Subtract one point for each error.)
[0-5]

______ Looks like a final product: neat and legible.
[1-5]

Public Speaking Evaluation Form

_______________________________________   _______________________________________
Speaker   Topic

______ Voice is strong, clear and loud enough to be heard easily.
[1-5]

______ Words are pronounced clearly and correctly.
[1-5]

______ Speech is slow enough to be easily understood. Uses pauses for emphasis.
[1-5]

______ Speaker maintains eye contact with audience. Facial expressions are appropriate to topic.
[1-5]

______ Posture is erect and body language shows confidence. Gestures are used for emphasis.
[1-5]

______ Ideas are presented in a logical order, with beginning, middle and end.
[1-5]

Public Speaking Evaluation Form

_______________________________________   _______________________________________
Speaker   Topic

______ Voice is strong, clear and loud enough to be heard easily.
[1-5]

______ Words are pronounced clearly and correctly.
[1-5]

______ Speech is slow enough to be easily understood. Uses pauses for emphasis.
[1-5]

______ Speaker maintains eye contact with audience. Facial expressions are appropriate to topic.
[1-5]

______ Posture is erect and body language shows confidence. Gestures are used for emphasis.
[1-5]

______ Ideas are presented in a logical order, with beginning, middle and end.
[1-5]

Public Speaking Evaluation Form

Speaker _______________________________   Topic _______________________________

	Excellent	Good	Needs Improvement	Weak
Voice: strong, clear and loud enough to be heard easily.				
Pronunciation: words are pronounced clearly and correctly.				
Pace: speech is slow enough to be easily understood; pauses for emphasis.				
Contact: speaker maintains eye contact with audience. Facial expressions are appropriate.				
Posture: body is erect; body language shows confidence. Gestures are used for emphasis.				
Content: ideas are presented in a logical order, with beginning, middle and end.				

Public Speaking Evaluation Form

Speaker _______________________________   Topic _______________________________

	Excellent	Good	Needs Improvement	Weak
Voice: strong, clear and loud enough to be heard easily.				
Pronunciation: words are pronounced clearly and correctly.				
Pace: speech is slow enough to be easily understood; pauses for emphasis.				
Contact: speaker maintains eye contact with audience. Facial expressions are appropriate.				
Posture: body is erect; body language shows confidence. Gestures are used for emphasis.				
Content: ideas are presented in a logical order, with beginning, middle and end.				

Notes

Notes